AF517100

Advance Praise for *Games Hospitals Play*

'*Games Hospitals Play* is an exposition of the grammar of healthcare inflation. It is important for both end users and policymakers to understand this script and for the latter to explore regulatory pathways that can deal with it. This is a crucial step in India's journey towards universal health coverage.'

Amitabh Kant, Former CEO,
NITI Aayog; India's ex-G20 Sherpa

'In *Games Hospitals Play*, Abantika Ghosh shines an outsider lens on insider perspectives about business practices of private hospitals. It is a must-read for all but most of all for policymakers who need to acknowledge, understand and deal with healthcare inflation urgently.'

C.K. Mishra, Former Secretary,
Ministry of Environment, Forest and Climate Change

'This book, by a sharply observant and incisively analytical health journalist with vast experience, profiles the many ways by which heavily invested and highly equipped private hospitals take advantage of trusting patients – inflating costs while avoiding accountability. By providing several real-life stories of patient experiences, doctors' insights, legal disputes, regulatory failures and false claims, the book becomes eminently readable besides carrying an assurance of unalloyed authenticity. After being cautioned about the many potholes on the road to private healthcare, the reader is also provided a very useful GPS that can guide a lay person's journey to safely reach the destination of appropriate and affordable healthcare.'

K. Srinath Reddy, Former Head of Cardiology,
AIIMS; Chancellor, PHFI University of Public Health Sciences

'In *Games Hospitals Play*, Abantika Ghosh casts a sharp and unflinching light on the hidden practices of India's private hospitals. Drawing on her long reporting experience and extensive fieldwork, she reveals how vulnerable patients are too often overcharged and underserved – while also highlighting the many ethical doctors who stand firm against these pressures. Her insights resonate with my own experience of engaging with the healthcare industry during the establishment of Ayushman Bharat PMJAY. This is a courageous, insightful and timely book that will not only empower patients but also challenge policymakers to strengthen regulation, accountability and trust in healthcare.'

Indu Bhushan, Former CEO,
National Health Authority

Games Hospitals Play

Decoding Your Private Healthcare Experience

ABANTIKA GHOSH

BLOOMSBURY

NEW DELHI • LONDON • OXFORD • NEW YORK • SYDNEY

BLOOMSBURY INDIA
Bloomsbury Publishing India Pvt. Ltd
Second Floor, LSC Building No. 4, DDA Complex, Pocket C – 6 & 7,
Vasant Kunj, New Delhi, 110070

BLOOMSBURY, BLOOMSBURY INDIA and the Diana logo
are trademarks of Bloomsbury Publishing Plc

First published in India 2025

Copyright © Abantika Ghosh, 2025

Abantika Ghosh has asserted her moral rights to be identified as the author of this work in accordance with the Indian Copyright Act, 1957

The views and opinions expressed in this book are the author's own and the publisher is in no way liable for the same

Some names and details of individuals have been changed to preserve their anonymity

All rights reserved. No part of this publication may be: i) reproduced or transmitted in any form, electronic or mechanical, including photocopying, recording or by means of any information storage or retrieval system without prior permission in writing from the publishers; or ii) used or reproduced in any way for the training, development or operation of artificial intelligence (AI) technologies, including generative AI technologies. The rights holders expressly reserve this publication from the text and data mining exception as per Article 4(3) of the Digital Single Market Directive (EU) 2019/790

Bloomsbury Publishing Plc does not have any control over, or responsibility for, any third-party websites referred to in this book. All internet addresses given in this book were correct at the time of going to press. The author and publisher regret any inconvenience caused if addresses have changed or sites have ceased to exist, but can accept no responsibility for any such changes

ISBN: HB: 978-93-61313-39-4; eBook: 978-93-61310-44-7
2 4 6 8 10 9 7 5 3 1

Typeset in Adobe Garamond by Manipal Technologies Limited
Printed and bound in India by Thomson Press India Ltd

MIX
Paper | Supporting responsible forestry
FSC® C010615

To find out more about our authors and books visit www.bloomsbury.com
and sign up for our newsletters

To Baba, who hated hospitals

Contents

Introduction

'Who is this book for?' asked a doctor friend, who works at a corporate hospital, when I shared a few chapters of this book with him. During my two decades as a health journalist, I have had numerous friends, colleagues and acquaintances approach me for advice on doctors and hospitals. Many of them requested me to 'put in a word' at a hospital or to intervene when something had not gone as expected. They were not asking for a discount. They were intimidated by the medical jargon, the anecdotes of catastrophic health spends, and were seeking reassurance that they would be assessed and treated fairly. They wanted to be spared over-investigation, unnecessary procedures and a prolonged hospital stay. In an ideal world, they would not have had to ask for a special intervention for something so basic.

The insecurity that people feel about Indian hospitals inspired this book. It is written for those who access private healthcare, with the aim of making them feel a little less lost and vulnerable. This book is also for policymakers, because this conversation really is a piece of the larger puzzle of healthcare in India. I have spent years talking with friends who work in the healthcare industry and have conducted detailed interviews with doctors in Kolkata, Delhi and Mumbai. These doctors either are currently working in the corporate sector or had worked there for some decades before moving out.

Not all of these doctors were open to contributing to such a book – some refused immediately, citing 'conflict of interest'. But many others spoke at length and shared case studies of actual incidents while dispassionately analysing why private healthcare has fallen into an inflationary spiral. Many doctors who have been quoted in this book are positioned at the apex of their profession. They work at elite institutions and are known for their personal adherence to ethics and medical norms.

Some of them asked to remain anonymous, for a myriad of reasons. Those who work at corporate hospitals exposed the business practices of their employers, because they did not agree with the notion that health is a business like any other. Others revealed some questionable practices of their friends and colleagues – people they routinely socialise with and, in some cases, have known from the time they were students.

I should note here that while many of the dubious practices happen with active or passive participation of doctors, it is my belief that the vast majority of doctors in this country still approach their profession with a desire to serve. And, like every profession, medicine has both good and bad practitioners. Some medical practitioners may be morally compromised, but for every doctor who is willing to bend the rules, there are many others who refuse to give up on their personal and professional integrity. It is the latter group that has made this book possible.

There are also variations in the way doctors approach their job. Even through disinterested decision-making, two doctors may differ in their handling of the same patient. One approach may prove to be better than the other, but it does not automatically follow that there are any ulterior motives behind their decisions.

The first rule of biology is that two plus two will almost never be four. This is because every living system is unique and, unlike machines, will react differently to the same external inputs. For a layperson, this concept is difficult to comprehend and that may affect their trust in doctors or the medical system.

In my research, I have often referred to the observations and orders of various courts, state and national commissions that have adjudicated upon complaints pertaining to corporate hospitals, obtaining the relevant documents using the Right to Information (RTI) Act and my professional network. Some are available online.

The clamour for adequate public health infrastructure to cater to India's formidable population has been so loud for so long that it has virtually eclipsed every other conversation in this space. One of the casualties of this obsession has been the regulation of the private sector in healthcare. It is perhaps justified, given that improvement of public health is one of the directive principles of state policy laid down in the Constitution of India. This conversation was rekindled by the Supreme Court in 2024, when it tasked the government with finding ways to regulate private hospital rates.[1] But the problem is like a demon that returns from the dead after every attempt to destroy it and has survived many past conversations about change.

The demand for a more rationalised price structure in healthcare has been raised for years by the insurance industry. It is now beginning to be voiced by upcoming managed care ventures too, which find themselves sandwiched between the government's notorious inertia in paying out monies owed under various public insurance programmes and the sharply rising costs of private healthcare. However, the argument that it is acceptable for market forces to decide costs in healthcare as they do in other sectors is inherently fallacious, because in no other sector is the consumer as vulnerable. The agency of a hospital on a lifesaving surgery cannot be equated to the choice of a brand to release a new refrigerator model.

There is also an unstated belief held by the government and the private healthcare system that they use to justify the lack of regulation of corporate hospital charges: if you choose private healthcare, you should be able to afford it and not need the government to intervene. This ignores the fact that if government hospitals do deliver quality healthcare, they often do so while compromising the dignity of the patient. Patients are required to navigate long queues and rude security staff to finally see a doctor. They have to sometimes wait for months for surgery. Citizens of Delhi are used to seeing patients and their families put up makeshift living arrangements on the pavements of Yusuf Sarai, around the All India Institute of Medical Sciences (AIIMS) hospital.

Besides, when private hospitals were getting established, many received incentives from the government on the condition that they would deliver healthcare to the poorer segments of the population as well. Multiple news reports over the years have exposed how that condition routinely goes unmet. When attempts are made to ensure compliance, the ensuing legal battle can go on for years.

When the Ayushman Bharat Pradhan Mantri Jan Arogya Yojana (PMJAY) was launched in 2018 with the intention to make private healthcare accessible to the poor, it received lukewarm participation from private hospitals. Of the estimated 44,000 private hospitals in the country, a measly 14,074 (as of 17 February 2025) are empanelled with the National Health Authority (NHA), which implements this flagship tertiary care programme of the NDA government.[2]

In the absence of any notable government initiative to regulate healthcare costs, it is left to the insurance companies to ask questions of private hospitals. But the poor penetration of health insurance and a host of other factors limit the potential of the insurance industry to serve as an effective check. In 2022, just over 51 crore people in the country had health insurance, mostly under government programmes such as PMJAY, Employees' State Insurance Corporation and the Central Government Health Scheme (CGHS).[3] These schemes set up pre-fixed rates. According to national survey data, only about 2 per cent of the population buys private insurance.

There are 40 crore people in the country with no health insurance whatsoever.[4] This category of people is referred to as the 'missing middle' – citizens whose incomes are high enough to make them ineligible for government insurance schemes but not enough to afford private health insurance. Until this section of people gets meaningful support for accessing quality healthcare in a dignified and affordable way, conversations about the business practices of private hospitals will stay relevant. However, the problem is barely acknowledged by policymakers, and that is why it has remained unaddressed for so long. The term 'missing middle' is a NITI Aayog coinage, but initiatives for the group are as yet limited to policy documents with little on-ground implementation.

This book ends with a rudimentary guide on what to watch out for when you are in a private hospital. It is not an exhaustive list, but it will, I hope, empower the patient and equip them to negotiate the corporate hospital space a little better. Structured information on medical practices is vital at a time when doctor–patient trust is at a nadir and every medical decision – even when taken solely for clinical reasons with no hidden motive for profit – is often suspect in the eyes of the patients or their families.

Unless we begin talking about the practices that are questionable, we taint vast swathes of the industry. This is unfair to all. Not being able to trust the individual whose decisions may mean life or death is a heavy burden indeed. It is also detrimental to the long-term outlook of India's healthcare system.

1

The MRP Trap

On Facebook, Ashutosh Singh's profile photo shows his twin daughters and him in the backdrop of the sea. It is an old photo, taken before 31 August 2017. That was the day when one of the twins, Durga, was admitted to a corporate hospital in Gurgaon with a bout of dengue. She was seven at the time. The little girl died in the hospital 15 days later. Even as the inconsolable parents mourned the loss of their daughter, the hospital handed them a bill of ₹16 lakh. Itemised in the bill were 611 syringes and 1,546 pairs of gloves.

Durga's parents later told the media and health ministry officials that the hospital had refused to release the girl's body unless the bill was paid in full. The hospital's stance, along with the outlandish numbers, triggered a public backlash. The health minister of India at the time was J.P. Nadda (who is back in office at the time of writing this book). He stepped in and promised action, even as the hospital issued a statement explaining that modern infection-control protocols require the use of a high number of consumables, especially when the patient is in the intensive care unit (ICU) as Durga had been.[1] It also listed the support that she had required during her stay in the facility – mechanical and high-frequency ventilation, continuous renal replacement therapy, intravenous antibiotics, inotropes, sedatives and analgesics.

There was a lot of noise about healthcare expenses in the aftermath of the incident but left no long-term effect on the sector. Eight years later, things remain the same. Outrage over high hospital bills periodically surfaces in our country and then dies a natural death with the change of the news cycle. That happened in the case of Durga too. Her family has since moved abroad.

A few weeks after Durga's death, a seven-year-old child died in another Gurgaon hospital. Shaurya Pratap Parmar was admitted for twelve days. After his death, his family was handed a bill of ₹15,88,429.[2] 'Shaurya was a beautiful boy. Brave,' reminisces Shaurya's father, Gopendra Parmar. 'He was in class four. When his health started deteriorating, the hospital referred him elsewhere, but within 24 hours he was gone.' Gopendra reveals that when he went to the state health minister for help, the minister responded: '*Tu garib aadmi hai to kya amir bana du tujhe* [if you are a poor man, do I need to make you rich]?' However, Union Minister Nadda wrote to the hospital 'requesting' them to refund the money. 'I did get a full refund,' says Gopendra. 'But my faith in doctors or the health system is gone forever. No matter which political party is in power, nobody wants to challenge private hospitals. Doctors, I feel, are worse than butchers.'[3] As Parmar's recollections of his exchange with the state minister show, the system has learned to look the other way when it comes to high costs of private healthcare.

Durga's death and the subsequent public outrage led to the emergence of an official government document that exposed the billing practices of private hospitals in shocking detail. The National Pharmaceutical Pricing Authority (NPPA) – the body that looks at the pricing of drugs and medical consumables in the country but in ordinary circumstances limits itself largely to items under price control – did an analysis of the bill that Durga's family had been given. The report has since been removed from the NPPA website, and I had to file an RTI request to get a copy.

The analysis found that an injection of paracetamol (the most commonly used medication to treat pain and fever), with a Maximum Retail Price (MRP) of ₹36.29, was billed at ₹310 per injection – a markup of 754 per cent. To a dose of a fibrinolytic agent (a medicine that helps with the breakdown of blood clots), with an MRP of ₹15.75, the hospital had added a margin of 343 per cent and billed it at ₹69.77, and for a pain medication called fentanyl, the hospital had charged ₹220 per dose to make a profit of 293 per cent on the MRP of ₹56.

Besides these, the hospital had billed dobutamine, an injectable medicine used to treat heart failure, at ₹287.50 per unit when the MRP was ₹28.75. This was a shocking markup of 914 per cent. The NPPA also found that the hospital had bought meropenem, a commonly used antibiotic, at ₹404.32 per injection but had added a margin of 670 per cent to bill it at ₹3,112 per unit. Most of these medicines are under price control which means that prices are regulated by the government through a periodically revised order. Medicines that are deemed essential are brought under price control to ensure that there is no unfettered profiteering on them. Manufacturers cannot list the MRP higher than the ceiling price fixed by the government. However, the hospital where Durga had been admitted had added a margin even for such medicines.

But the biggest markups were found in consumables. For a 10 ml syringe with an MRP of ₹3.26, the hospital had charged ₹37 – a markup of 1,035 per cent. A three-way stopcock bi-valve, used for giving multiple infusions through a common tube so that there are less needle pricks, that had cost the hospital ₹5.77, was marked up by 1,737 per cent and billed at ₹106 per unit. The hospital had also charged ₹115 for an intravenous (IV) infusion set bought for ₹8.39 – a 1,271 per cent margin – and ₹75 per pair of surgical gloves sold at ₹9.86, which came to a markup of 661 per cent.

A few months later, the NPPA released another report that found similar inflationary pricing practices at four other hospitals in Delhi.[4] But nothing much was done afterwards, and the reports have since been removed from the organisation's website.

Even when private hospitals bill at MRP, they are almost always making a profit. That is because the procurement price is usually significantly less than the marked MRP. In fact, the difference between the procurement price and the MRP often determines which brand of medicine a pharmacy chooses to stock. This markup is also among the reasons why corporate hospitals do not allow medicines to be procured from outside. However, they justify this policy by stating that the quality of medicines sold outside their own pharmacy cannot be trusted.

One can argue that keeping a small margin for consumables is standard business practice and is not unique to the healthcare industry. Hotels, restaurants, beauty salons and automobile service centres all do it. The difference is that none of these other industries can be classified as essential to life. It is possible to survive without a facial or a fancy brunch but not without treatment during a health emergency.

Orders galore, little action

The billing practices of private hospitals underwent an unprecedented, albeit short-lived, scrutiny after the tragic deaths of Durga and Shaurya in 2017. However, these dubious practices had been exposed earlier too. Strictures had already been passed against the coercive practice of forcing patients to pay MRP for drugs that had been procured at discounted bulk rates. Back in 2014, the National Consumer Disputes Redressal Commission had pointed out in no uncertain terms that this practice took advantage of a patient's vulnerability.[5]

In 2009, there was the case of Meenu Jain. She was suffering from Guillain-Barre Syndrome (GBS), a rare neurological disorder in which the immune system, unable to recognise what is its own and what is foreign, starts attacking the body's own nerves. In mild forms it only presents itself as some transient muscle weakness, but in severe cases it can cause total muscular paralysis. Sometimes patients are unable to even breathe unassisted. When Meenu was admitted to Fortis Escort hospital in Jaipur, she was advised to undergo a treatment of Iviglob EX injections for five days. The hospital billed each injection at ₹18,990. The same injection was being sold 30 per cent to 40 per cent cheaper at pharmacies outside the hospital.

At the end of the hospitalisation period, Meenu was presented with a bill of ₹6,82,965. When Meenu's husband, Prem Chand Jain, asked for details, such as the batch number and cost price of the injections, the hospital did not provide the information. The matter reached the national commission via the district and state forums, both of which agreed that the complainant had been overcharged. The commission ruled that though the complainant had signed the consent and the counselling form, it was also important to understand the state of mind of the complainant.

Prem Chand Jain's wife was in a critical condition, which meant that the hospital was in a position of power. It did not permit him to purchase the Iviglob EX injections from outside, despite repeated verbal requests. This meant that the hospital authorities had indirectly imposed unjustifiable and unreasonable conditions on Jain. The hospital's argument that it had done so to ensure the quality and genuineness of the drugs failed to pass muster with the commission.

The injections in question had been sold at MRP by the hospital. So as per norms, there had not actually been any overcharging by the hospital. However, the commission was of the view that given the seriousness of the disease and the critical condition of the patient and the knowledge that it is standard trade practice for bulk buyers of expensive medicines to be given a discount, the hospital should have allowed at least marginal discount of about 10 per cent to 20 per cent. The commission held that as the drugs had been procured at a much lower cost by the hospital, there was already an adequate margin of profit and corporate hospitals should not be commercial or business centres profiteering from the exploitation of critical patients. It ordered a refund of 50 per cent of the excess amount charged.

But the case remained an isolated one with no lasting systemic change stemming from it. There were no attempts by the government to regulate private hospitals or bring in guidelines to prevent profiteering off life-saving medications. In the meantime, hospitals have worked out newer ways of boosting bottom lines by making the patient pay for not just medicines and medical consumables but also even toiletries, sometimes charging several times the cost of the item. In 2015, an individual had approached the Competition Commission of India (CCI) with a complaint against Max Hospital, pointing out that a syringe with a marked MRP of ₹11.50 – available outside the hospital for ₹10 – was being sold by the hospital from its in-house pharmacy for ₹19.50. The complainant, citing the dominant position Max has in the market, had accused it of predatory pricing.

The CCI did not disagree. It observed that once a patient is admitted in the hospital, they don't have any option to purchase the product from the open market. The commission alleged that the hospital, in connivance with the manufacturer of the syringe, was charging a higher price by unfairly printing a higher MRP on the syringe sold at the hospital. The CCI was convinced that the syringe sold by the hospital was identical in quality and design to the one sold outside the hospital at a lower marked MRP. It dismissed the argument of the hospital that the syringe available in the open market was different from the product sold by the hospital in its usefulness at the time of surgery. Accordingly, the CCI declared in an order dated 17 November 2015 that Max Healthcare, owner and operator of Max Hospital, was in violation of the provision of section 4(2)(a)(ii) of the Competition Act, 2002.[6]

Section 4(2)(a)(ii) of the Act states that if a business entity indulges in price manipulation in buying and selling of goods, it can constitute an abuse of a dominant position. The CCI asked for an inquiry into the matter by the Director General (DG) Office, which is the investigative wing of the commission. The report of the DG was equally damning for the healthcare behemoth. While the report failed to substantiate the allegation that Max Healthcare had entered into a formal understanding with the syringe manufacturer to print inflated MRPs, it took into consideration factors such as number of beds, doctors and patients at the hospital and the financial heft of the organisation to conclude that Max indeed held a dominant position in the market.

The CCI order dated 31 August 2018 noted, referencing the DG's report, that Max Healthcare had earned huge profit margins ranging from 269.84 per cent to 527 per cent in the financial year 2014–15 and from 276.96 per cent to 527 per cent in the financial year 2015–16 by sale of different syringes.[7] It also found merit in the DG's observation that with the aim of earning more profit, the organisation had moved from purchasing flow-wrap syringes to procuring blister-pack syringes during the financial year 2015–16. Max Healthcare was also found to be compelling its in-patients to purchase products only from its in-house pharmacy.

The DG's report also concluded that this practice was in contravention of the provisions of Section 4(2)(a)(ii) of the Competition Act. Noting that the practice of 'exploitative pricing' for 'locked-in patients' is followed by most hospitals, the CCI then asked for the ambit of the investigation to be widened beyond just the sale of syringes in hospitals. It also recommended that the DG investigate other 'super-specialty' hospitals.

The expanded DG report covered twelve such hospitals in Delhi NCR, including Apollo, Max, Fortis, Sir Ganga Ram, Batra and St Stephen's. It came to the conclusion that all of them abused their positions of dominance by charging 'unfair and excessive prices' for room rent, medicines, medical tests, medical devices and consumables.[8] Max subsequently challenged the CCI proceedings in the Delhi High Court. The case is ongoing.[9]

The MRP sleight

Drug MRPs hide more than they reveal. Except for a few medicines that are considered 'essential', and with the list periodically revised, most drugs are not under price control. Therefore, the marked price of a drug accounts for commissions paid at every step in the supply chain, from the manufacturer and distributor to the stockist and pharmacist. This leaves room for sizeable discounts if a link of the chain could be removed or the amount of commission reduced.

This is illustrated by the pricing of medicines by some pharmacists – such as Nath Brothers in New Friends Colony in Delhi as well as the shops that line the road outside AIIMS – that offer 10 per cent to

50 per cent discounts on the MRP. They keep a lower percentage as their own commission, but the resultant increase in the volume of sales makes up for this reduction. Such chemists become the preferred shops for patients who are on long-term or expensive treatments, such as chemotherapy for cancer patients or monoclonal antibodies for infectious or chronic diseases. These expensive medications even when administered to admitted patients are sometimes not covered by health insurance plans; there are hardly any plans that reimburse drug costs for patients who are not in hospital.

Pharmacists buy in bulk, which is partly why they can afford to give discounts. But corporate hospital chains may buy even bigger quantities and do centralised procurement for multiple sites. Yet, these hospitals almost always sell medicines at MRP. It is not illegal to sell medicines at MRP, but it is a practice that is perceived as a major factor in healthcare inflation. Corporate hospitals also avoid prescribing drugs under price control as much as possible. A report by the National Pharmaceutical Pricing Authority found that drugs under price control make up a measly 4 per cent of hospital bills while unscheduled drugs that are not under price control make up 25 per cent.[10]

For bulk buyers such as hospitals, the marked MRP of a drug can even be the deciding factor in choosing the brand of medicine to be procured. A manufacturer who marks a lower MRP for a drug may lose out to another manufacturer charging a higher MRP for the same product – not because their drug is of inferior quality but because they are offering a lower commission to the retailer (in this case the hospital) for selling that drug to the end customer. The information disparity that exists between the doctor and the patient drives sales. The patient who is the end user has no say on what medicines to take; they have no option but to trust the doctor. In mandating that medicines for hospitalised patients must be procured from the in-house pharmacy, even though there are cheaper options, that trust is exploited to boost bottom lines.

An interesting inversion of this insistence on the in-house pharmacy is seen in case of free patients. In states such as Delhi, many private hospitals were given free or subsidised land with the catch that 10 per cent to 33 per cent of the beds would be reserved for patients coming from economically weaker sections. These patients would not pay for the services but had to be given the same level of care and attention as the other paying patients. This was never a provision that the hospitals welcomed. There have been several litigations on the matter, with hospitals offering various reasons why it was not possible to offer equal treatment to patients who did not pay. One nasty sticking point was drugs. Some hospitals went to court saying they could provide free beds and medical treatments but could not provide free medicines.[11]

Organisations such as Social Jurist – headed by Delhi High Court lawyer Ashok Aggarwal – work to uphold the right of the poor to access facilities at hospitals that have received massive exemptions from the government and are expected to deliver healthcare on a 'no profit no loss' basis in return. They have so far been successfully thwarted by the hospitals on the matter of providing free drugs and consumables. Thus, for these non-paying patients, the contention that the only trustworthy source of medicine is the in-house pharmacy is conveniently bypassed. This can mean two things – none flattering for these hospitals – hospitals are either not equally committed to the health and well-being of all patients, regardless of their paying capacity, or there are concerns other than quality when making it mandatory for regular patients to buy medicines from the hospital pharmacy.

Aggarwal says, 'In Delhi, many private hospitals are mandated to reserve 10 per cent of their beds for free patients, whereas a major name such as Apollo is mandated to reserve a third of its beds. But the hospitals found a loophole in the contract, which meant that they did not have to provide free patients with drugs.' This causes a lot of financial stress to these patients. 'We have been fighting for this to be changed since 1997, but so far, the hospitals have not budged. In 2009, the Delhi High Court had directed Apollo Hospital to include free drugs and consumables in the treatment of lower-income patients. But the hospital got a stay on that order from the Supreme Court,' he adds. Aggarwal says that the high court judgement had not only given unambiguous directions on the services non-paying patients would be entitled to at hospitals but had also made some observations about the pricing of drugs and consumables that indicated that not all was above board. The judgement noted that it was 'disturbing' that the figures submitted by the hospital declared the expenditure on consumables and medicines as ₹186 crore out of the total revenue of ₹391.19 crore. It also highlighted, for perspective, the fact that G.B. Pant Hospital, a super-specialty institution with 600 beds, run by the government of Delhi, spent only around ₹23 crore on consumables and medicines in 2008.

The petitioner, All India Lawyers Union (Delhi chapter), contended that the promoters of Apollo Hospital had set up front companies from which consumables and medicines were being bought at a very high rate. This was vehemently disputed by the hospital. The judgment concluded: 'We do not wish to express any opinion on this aspect except that the government will enquire into this aspect and ascertain whether such high expenditure is justified.' There have been several governments in Delhi since this order but not one has conducted this inquiry.

For some years now, India has been debating the concept of promoting generic medicines instead of branded ones to lower healthcare costs. The Indian Medical Council (Professional Conduct, Etiquette and Ethics) Regulations, 2002 states that every physician should prescribe drugs with generic names instead of branded names. This means that instead of prescribing a 'Calpol' or a 'Dolo', the prescription should read 'paracetamol' – the name of the salt that is present in both these drugs. Generic medicines are usually cheaper because the marketing costs that companies incur are factored into the MRP of branded medicines. A famous brand will usually be more expensive than one that is not as well known even if there is no difference in the costs of developing and manufacturing the product for the two companies.

The National Medical Commission (NMC) Act, 2019 empowers the appropriate state medical councils, or the Ethics and Medical Registration Board (EMRB) of the Commission, to take disciplinary action against a doctor for not following this rule. However, when the NMC published its Registered Medical Practitioner (Professional Conduct) Regulations, 2023, such was the furore about the clause which reiterated that doctors should only use generic names in prescriptions that the regulations were kept in abeyance. Both the Indian Medical Association – the apex body of medical practitioners – and the Indian Pharmaceutical Alliance – a trade body comprising some of the most prominent Indian drug companies – were up in arms against the regulation because of what they called 'concerns about the quality of drugs'.[12]

That is also the argument that corporate hospitals use when shunning generic drug use. But for many charitable or trust hospitals, the first strategy to bring down healthcare costs is to use generic medicine. I spoke to a senior functionary of a prominent charitable hospital in South Delhi on this. The official – who wishes to remain unnamed – has also worked in the government and corporate sectors. 'The business and profit aspects for us are different as charitable hospitals,' they explained, 'so we have a lot more scope to deliver healthcare at cost price or at a small markup. But even then, we have to look for ways to keep expenses down. Therefore, we use generic drugs in the hospital as far as possible. For the branded medicines that are used, we do not charge at MRP but at a price that is closer to what we pay to procure them.'

Drug dilemmas for outpatients

Margins are exorbitant at hospital pharmacies. But the prices of drugs in the open market are not for the faint-hearted either. In India, there are guidelines in existence for prescription audits (the periodic examination of random prescriptions to check for drug overuse or abuse) and standard treatment guidelines that lay down the drugs, diagnostics and treatment modules by specialty.

However, in the absence of statutory backing, these guidelines are not uniformly followed. Doctors practising independently are guided by their own scruples/competence with little oversight. For outpatients at hospitals, it is the sole discretion of the doctor in the outpatient department (OPD), who may be a relatively junior person, over what medicines are to be used and for how long.

A senior doctor at a private hospital in Delhi, who started off at a government teaching hospital and worked there for many years before making the shift, says that if one looks carefully at most prescriptions given by an average doctor in a big city – regardless of whether they are affiliated to a private hospital or have a standalone practice – they will usually be fairly long. Most would be drugs that are not under price control; there will be things like vitamins and supplements prescribed that may not immediately come across as essential. In some cases, doctors prescribe these to patients who can afford them in order to get free samples from the manufacturer that they can then give to poorer patients. 'But there may be other considerations too,' he admits.

He adds that pharmaceutical companies sometimes ingratiate themselves with doctors not through gifts and incentives but by sponsoring seminars that doctors attend as part of their continuing medical education (CME). CME sessions and seminars are a great outreach option for pharmaceutical companies as they can reach out to doctors from more than one department. Most departments have at least one seminar a week; sometimes they are held at fancy hotels. There is also scope for more personalised perks for individual doctors. To tackle this issue, in March 2024 the government of India notified a uniform code of marketing practices for pharmaceutical companies that prohibits them from sponsoring trips for doctors or their families – whether in India or abroad – unless they are speakers at an event. Neither can the companies conduct CMEs outside the country.[13]

If doctors were to not name a medicine by their brands, then it would give the patient a choice of buying a drug based on either the price or their perception of the manufacturer. However, one of the arguments against this is that it may leave patients at the mercy of chemists, who have less accountability than doctors and may decide the brand based solely on the margins of their commission and not quality. Regardless, the generic prescription regulation is never followed as doctors claim that the efficacy of various brands of the same medicine can differ, and hence they would not want to risk their reputation by leaving the choice to the chemist or the patient.

Thus, the challenge with such regulations lies in their implementation. In absence of prescription audits, the only option to monitor trends of drug use is through drug sales at pharmacies. But current laws do not require chemists to save all prescriptions they fill. Also, the Central Drugs and Standards Control Authority (CDSCO) and its state counterparts are severely understaffed. They struggle to even control the practice of selling prescription-only medications over the counter.

Ensuring the prescription of generic drugs though is not the mandate of the CDSCO, but of the NMC. But the commission does not have the field inspectors required for such an exercise. There is also no mechanism for proactively monitoring engagements between pharmaceutical companies and individual doctors or their departments. It is not difficult for multinational corporations to organise opportunities for doctors to be speakers at events held at foreign locales, thereby allowing them to sponsor such trips. The margins in drug MRPs take care of these 'overhead' expenses. But the price of all such transgressions is eventually paid by the patient. Doctors play the most important role in this system, holding the key to most healthcare decisions, but are not the sole reason for inflationary pressures. That vein runs deep and is symptomatic of a systemic malaise.

Economist Kenneth Arrow argues in his seminal paper that in an industry where outcomes are as uncertain as they are in healthcare, information is a commodity that is being sold.[14] Based on that information, we need to assess the quality of the services provided by the very people who are giving us that information.

Without adequate and complete information, we would not be able to do that assessment. It makes sense for the people that have access to information, to dispense it in a way that is most suited for their purposes. Therefore, the business of healthcare must not be left to market forces. Arrow writes that the value of the information is usually not known in any meaningful sense to the buyer.

'If, indeed, he knew enough to measure the value of the information, he would know the information itself,' he argues. But it is this information, in the form of skilled care, that is being bought from doctors. 'The illusive character of information as a commodity suggests that it departs considerably from the usual marketability assumptions about commodities,' Arrow concludes. Indeed, in the five decades since the publication of his hypothesis, the business of healthcare has continued to be built on the firm pillar of this information bias.

Medicine procurement in the government sector

It would be a gross falsehood to say that profit motive in healthcare is limited only to the private sector or that morally questionable activities and practices exclusively exist there. Private hospitals account for over 60 per cent of the health infrastructure in India. But government hospitals are also complicit in healthcare corruption and in adding to the financial burden of expensive drugs and consumables faced by the consumer. The difference is only in execution. Like private hospitals, government hospitals also have pharmacies that are expected to supply all the drugs prescribed to a patient at no cost. However, that does not always happen.

Commonly used drugs go mysteriously missing from hospital pharmacies even when nearby pharmacies are well stocked. Patients end up having to buy drugs that they are entitled to receive for free. Equally mysteriously, the income of hospital staff shows a steady upward trend.[15] Drug shortages in government hospital pharmacies have been a persistent problem, and over the years several committees have recommended ways to deal with the issue.

In April 2024, a committee headed by noted gastroenterologist Dr S.K. Sarin had submitted to the Delhi High Court recommendations on how to improve the functioning of Delhi government hospitals. The committee had recommended that hospitals maintain a minimum inventory of two months of the drugs listed in the essential drug list as well as commonly used consumables. It also asked for hospitals to have ready-made rate contracts to meet up to 50 per cent of the annual demand so that the tendering process for rate contracts may be initiated in due time to ensure that there is a secure supply of medicines and consumables for six months.[16]

Even the Central Government Health Services (CGHS) – a healthcare programme for government employees and some other beneficiary groups that has defined primary, secondary and tertiary care components – is not immune to such unexplained shortages. The Comptroller and Auditor General of India, in its 2022 report titled 'Performance Audit of Procurement and Supply of Drugs in CGHS', noted that the CGHS wellness centres suffered from persistent drug shortages thanks to tardy procurement. 'Against the annual requirement of 1,169 drugs in CGHS, there were only 6 to 290 drugs available in wellness centres,' the report noted.[17]

There are other issues too. Because of a procurement rule that mandates government organisations to buy only from the entity that quotes the lowest prices, these pharmacies sometimes end up getting drugs of dubious quality. Occasionally, government hospital doctors will ask patients to avoid the free medicines from the hospital's pharmacy and instead buy them from outside, because they have found that patients do not always respond adequately to the drugs stocked by the in-house pharmacy. Last year, the home ministry launched an inquiry into allegations of substandard drugs being supplied at three Delhi government hospitals.[18]

Regulating drug prices is tricky because in the absence of adequate checks there could be compromises made on quality. It could also mean that a drug put under price control becomes economically unviable for manufacturers and completely disappears from the market. This was seen in 2001, when aspirin – which is a staple not just as a pain medication but also as a blood thinner in elderly patients – disappeared from pharmacy shelves after a series of regulations made it impossible for companies to continue manufacturing it.[19] Then, in 2014, a range of medicines used for the treatment of diabetes and acne became unavailable after they were brought under price control.[20]

But the repercussions of not keeping a check on prices are also grave. In the non-medical world, the MRP is the benchmark of ethical business practice. The occasional storms in teacups over how much a can of coke costs in the airport lounge bear testimony to how price sensitive we are as people. But in an arena where much more than just money is at stake, and where quality can mean the difference between life and death, that very principle is turned on its head, reducing MRPs to just another marketing ruse that allows big corporate players to call the shots and bend the market to suit their interests.

In the 1980s, when the world saw a gradual rightward shift to the policies of Ronald Reagan in the US and Margaret Thatcher in the UK, the belief in the omniscience of markets was profound. Jury is still out on the long-term effects of some of those policies, but by following a similar principle in healthcare, we are risking runaway inflation.

2

One Surgery for the Price of Two

Rakesh, a 53-year-old businessman from Faridabad, had a chronic cardiac condition that was being treated at a posh private hospital in Delhi. After going to that hospital for years, it had become familiar. His experience had been good there, and he trusted his cardiologist. So when his wife was advised a gallbladder surgery, that hospital was the natural choice. The hospital gave him an estimate of ₹2.30 lakh for the surgery.

Rakesh thought that it was reasonable and knew that he could pay that amount with some help from his extended family. The surgery went well. But when the bill came, it was a rude shock. The total came to ₹3.90 lakh. Rakesh was prepared for some escalation, but this was way beyond his expectation, particularly because there had been no complications and the surgery had gone as planned. He had already asked everyone he knew for money.

His cardiologist spoke to me about the case. He would like to remain anonymous as he continues to work at the same hospital. 'One day Rakesh burst into my office,' he recalls. 'He was hysterical. He showed me the bill and said that there was no way he could pay this money. As an educated man he understood that an almost 69 per cent increase in the bill without any major complication was not possible, and he was convinced that there was some mistake.' The doctor calmed him down and examined the bill, only to find that he had been charged for cholecystectomy (removal of the gallbladder) and also for adhesiolysis – the removal of scar tissue around organs which forms as part of the body's natural healing processes. The two procedures had been billed as separate surgeries, with all items – including the operation theatre (OT) charges and the surgeon's fee – being counted twice.

'This was ridiculous,' says the cardiologist. 'It is possible for some fibrous tissues to grow around an organ and if that had happened in this case, the surgeon would obviously have to remove those adhesions before removing the organ. But the fact is that the surgeon had only performed one surgery and the OT had only been used once. How could they be billed separately?' The doctor immediately took it up with the hospital management, flagging it as an unfair business practice. Only when he threatened to reveal it to the media were the charges reversed.

To this day, neither Rakesh nor his cardiologist know whether adhesiolysis had really been required in his wife's case or whether it was just a regular gallbladder removal procedure that had been dressed up to earn the hospital some extra money. It is true that adhesiolysis is required more often for women, but that does not mean that every woman needs it. Rakesh had been lucky to have someone on the inside who understood the way of the hospital and who was willing to take up the cudgels on his behalf. But many are not that lucky.

The practice of adding an extra procedure to the bill in addition to the originally planned surgery is not uncommon in private hospitals. It increases the potential earnings from surgeries such as adenoidectomy (removal of adenoids) and hysterectomy (removal of uterus) that are otherwise relatively affordable. Adhesiolysis is a popular choice for this purpose because adhesions can develop anywhere (they are more common in the abdomen) and pre-surgical imaging or other tests may not reveal their presence. They are often discovered only when the patient is in the OT and the surgeon has to make an impromptu decision on whether to remove them or not. Post-surgery, nobody other than those present in the OT during the surgery would know what transpired inside. However, even if adhesiolysis is required, it is not an isolated procedure that can be shown as a separate surgery.

Another common procedure that has scope for artificially inflated bills is haemorrhoidectomy (removal of piles). A senior executive at a corporate hospital, who is also a clinician by training and has practised medicine for some years, tells me that nobody other than the doctor can know the number of haemorrhoids present. 'Sometimes they can claim there were internal and external haemorrhoids and that they had to be managed differently – one removed, another treated with sclerotherapy (injection to the blood vessel to manage an abnormality) and so on,' she reveals. 'The bill for that one procedure can increase several times because of this. Sometimes they will also add a charge for examination under anaesthesia. But the surgery was done under anaesthesia anyway, so how can there be a separate charge for the examination?'

The executive is quick to add that the approach to billing differs from doctor to doctor. In some cases, the doctor does their best to keep the costs reasonable. However, hospitals have now added corporate layers between the clinical and billing departments comprising management professionals who tally various aspects of patient care with the final bill to plug any gaps.

At big corporate hospitals, most low-cost surgeries are now done through a laparoscopic procedure, in which a small camera is inserted through a hole. An excised organ is also brought out through the latter. But whether it is laparoscopic or an open surgery, it is impossible for a patient or their family to keep track of what happens in the OT. In fact, they cannot even verify whether the doctor they have been speaking to (and paying for) performs the surgery or if the procedure is delegated to a junior surgeon.

Even after tightened corporate control over billing, it is possible for surgeons to exert some calming influence on the bill. One of the ways they do so is by editing out some consumables or equipment that may have been used. For example, there is a device called Harmonic that is used to cut tissue and seal the site of the cut with ultrasonic rays to control bleeding and another called Ligasure, which can help fuse cut tissue. When used in the OT, these are charged separately. 'A surgeon who is mindful of costs will sometimes use them but not mention it when they are filling in the billing codes,' explains a surgeon at a private hospital in Delhi. 'There may also be more than one way of doing the same surgery. The surgeon may choose a procedure that is more expensive only because it was required for a certain case but then fill in the code for a cheaper procedure. This is still quite common.' However, the room for such magnanimity is now shrinking. Sometimes the extra procedure that is billed is not even a standalone procedure. For example, a diagnostic laparoscopy (in which a keyhole camera is used to see inside the body) may be clubbed with appendicectomy. The patient has no way of finding out if a keyhole camera, apart from the one used for removing the appendix, was indeed inserted for exploration purposes. Most don't bother with the details if the doctor says the magic words: 'We looked around and found nothing. You are hale and hearty.'

A senior gastrointestinal surgeon at a prominent hospital chain in North India reveals that the decision on whether a patient needs an exploratory surgery is heavily dependent on the examining doctor. 'It is based on their reading of the reports,' he says. 'There is a fine line between clinical discretion and a decision that is taken with something other than the patient's best interests in mind. That line is not easy to discern.' In this age of preventive health check-ups, it is common to find an unnatural growth in some part of the body in an apparently asymptomatic individual. All it takes is the word 'cancer' and patients automatically agree to whatever option the doctor certifies as 'best'. 'In exploratory surgery, you do not know what you will find and the best result is to not find anything,' says the surgeon. 'With that, the patient, the surgeon and the hospital are all happy. One because they have been declared healthy and the others because they have managed to raise a fat invoice.'

Surgical costs may also go up if doctors do not follow established conventions. There are some conditions for which surgery is recommended in phases. The hospital executive also adds, 'For example, when repairing a perforation of the ileum (the lowermost part of the intestine), the recommended approach is to first make a small hole in the upper part of the intestine for the exit of faecal matter while bypassing the affected portion. This procedure is called colostomy. Once the ileum has recovered, a second surgery is done to repair the hole. But some surgeons may not follow this process. They may repair the perforation at the very outset.' If this is done to a patient with already thinned intestinal walls, the patient inevitably returns with another perforation. 'Only then is the recommended approach taken. So instead of two procedures, the patient needs three,' the executive explains.

Occasionally, the senior management of the hospital will also tactfully point out to doctors that they have not got as many patients into surgery as required or that the surgeries that they did perform have not generated as much revenue as the hospital would have liked.

Over time the breakup of surgery costs have also changed significantly. Earlier, the surgeon's fees and the hospital charges (minus the cost of the hospital stay) used to be about the same, with each receiving an equal share of the total surgery fee. During the last couple of decades, new charges and new billing ideas have been introduced, which have led to a widening chasm between the two. According to doctors who have experienced this transition, while the hospital's share has increased by 100 per cent to 200 per cent, the surgeon's remuneration per operation has seen only a 40 per cent to 50 per cent increase. So, the bulk of the surgery fee now goes to the hospital and not the person who performs it.

Thanks to taxi-hailing apps such as Uber and Ola, the concept of surge pricing is very well understood. It is the practice of increasing fares during times of high demand for cabs, such as during office rush hours or festivals. It is the premium that can be charged in a market where demand outstrips supply. However, many hospitals have now begun using the surge-pricing concept to inflate surgical bills.[1] The concept is relatively new in the healthcare industry and one that is causing a lot of angst both for patients and health insurers.

In surge pricing in healthcare, corporate hospitals have adopted the concept of 'peak charges' for OTs during the time of the day when there is high demand.[2] Along with other arbitrary billing practices, this may have added a 20 per cent premium to India's healthcare inflation, which is already very high at 14 per cent. This means that even routine surgical procedures such as hysterectomies and cholecystectomies are seeing an increase in fees for procedures done during the day. If the patient agrees to have surgery at night, they can avoid the peak charge. However, in a non-emergency situation, this is hardly possible because it would also require the doctors, nurses and other OT staff to work at odd hours.

Patient choice and overtreatment

The internet and private health insurance providers have given patients greater choice and flexibility. They can now choose the procedure or treatment they want and sometimes even go 'doctor-shopping' to find a medical professional who would agree with their chosen option even if it is unnecessary or more expensive. However, not all surgeons are willing to sacrifice clinical judgement to heed patient requests.

A Kolkata-based urologist, who trained at a government medical college and is now working in a private hospital, tells me about the time a well-heeled patient came to him with an inflamed prostate. After doing the necessary tests, he found that there were stones in the gland. His clinical discretion told him that the patient did not need to undergo surgery and could manage the condition with medication. However, the medication for prostate stones may sometimes become a lifelong requirement. The patient went away unhappy with the proposed treatment. However, he was back after a few months.

'It turns out that the man was daunted by the prospect of being on medications for the rest of his life,' says the urologist, 'so he travelled to Chennai, where a doctor readily performed the surgery.'

However, the patient then developed strictures, which is a common post-surgery complication associated with prostate surgery. 'There is always a chance of a complication in a medical procedure,' adds the urologist, 'so the best approach is to do it only when essential. But to be fair, individual assessments differ over the circumstances in which surgery would be considered as the best option.'

The urologist concedes that surgeons who are paid hefty salaries by private hospitals always feel the pressure of targets and numbers. 'If the doctor is working as a consultant, the pressure is much less because the hospital does not pay a fixed monthly sum to consultants,' he explains. 'Instead, the hospital takes a cut from the doctor's fee for letting them use their facilities. For every surgery a consultant does, the hospital also makes money by charging OT fees or for consumables or staff. The surgeon takes his fees based on the work he does. But a lot of newer hospitals are hiring doctors as employees and paying them big salaries. These doctors then have the pressure of numbers.'

The practice of 'surprise billing' in surgeries is fairly well documented in medical literature abroad but not so much in India. In 2020, a study published in *JAMA* estimated that one in five patients get an unexpected bill after surgery.[3] Not all these cases are unethical. During surgery, there are many snap decisions that may need to be taken, sometimes to save a life. Those procedures can add to the bill. But it is a tad naive to suggest that all decisions that are taken in the OT or outside it are lifesaving ones with no financial implications for the surgeon or the hospital. It is important that doctors and hospitals make money to pay their bills, sustain and expand their business and keep abreast of latest medical technologies and developments. But patients too need to be able to access medical care without facing the prospect of bankruptcy.

There are also variables such as administrative costs, overheads, equipment, consumables, insurance and legal costs that can cause the cost of the same surgery to vary widely from hospital to hospital. These are some of the reasons that various hospitals cite to justify their inability to have fixed charges for surgery when asked to do so; that argument may again be rehashed when the government starts action on the Supreme Court direction to the government to fix hospital charges. In a 2013 paper published in *The BMJ*, Dr Sushmita Chatterjee and Dr Ramanan Laxminarayan of the Public Health Foundation of India looked at the costs of some common procedures done at a wide spectrum of hospitals – a 57-bed charitable hospital, a 200-bed private hospital, a 400-bed district hospital, a 655-bed private teaching hospital and a 778-bed tertiary care teaching hospital.[4] The purpose of the study was primarily to inform the reimbursement rates prescribed by the Rashtriya Swasthya Bima Yojana (RSBY), a small-scale insurance programme that used to be run by the labour ministry for workers in the informal sector.

The authors of the paper found that the cost of conducting a caesarean section ranged from ₹2,469 to ₹41,087, a hysterectomy from ₹4,124 to ₹57,622 and an appendectomy from ₹2,421 to ₹3,616. To better understand where those numbers may stand today, consider that a dollar stands at ₹88 (at the time of writing this book) as opposed to ₹52 – the exchange rate at the time this analysis was undertaken. The authors observed that even though the operational costs of the surgical units of the charitable hospital and the private teaching hospital were not significantly different, there were huge differences in the average cost per procedure: ₹41,607 at the charitable hospital versus ₹5,958 at the private teaching hospital.

Dr Chatterjee is now associated with the George Institute of Global Health. She explains that there are many factors that decide how a hospital bills surgical procedures. 'In my work I have found that location is a very important determinant,' she reveals. 'At a more expensive location, the building rent would significantly increase the cost of running the hospital.' Another reason she cites is the efficiency of the system, explaining that the more the facilities are used, the less will be the per-unit cost. 'During COVID-19 pandemic when I was doing my research for a paper, I found that in one particular hospital, it was the cost of the plumbing that was extremely high,' she says. 'That had the biggest effect on treatment costs.' However, she believes that it should not be the government but the hospital management that should review, fix and rationalise rates.

While medicine is evolving based on emerging scientific ideas, billing practices of corporate hospitals are metamorphosing towards more profits. The billing – which is the act of recording the relevant code assigned to procedures, materials and equipment in the documentation – is done by doctors. Increasingly now, doctors find themselves answerable to a group of administrators hired to ensure that the hospital makes the most profits out of existing resources and manpower. This means that they are sometimes constrained in making concessions even for their own colleagues or immediate family members. Before this revamp of the system, doctors had the discretion to write prescriptions or advise surgeries in a way that the bills would be more affordable.

A resident doctor at a private hospital reveals that a surgeon would sometimes carry out the required procedure but bill for a cheaper operation if the patient couldn't afford it. 'When I took the father of a close friend for treatment for a bleed in his brain, my senior asked us how much they could pay,' he recalls. 'Then in the documentation he noted a procedure that suited the patient's budget, but in the OT he did what was necessary to save the patient. The procedure he performed would have cost much more than the one he had written in the files. He saved my friend a few lakhs with this simple gesture.'

But now such generosity is becoming increasingly difficult as management professionals prowl the corridors, the wards and the OTs to find out what surgeries are being done and what equipment is in use. If the code given by the doctor is different from their own lists, they make the necessary changes in the final bill. A senior doctor at a corporate hospital in South Delhi recently found this the hard way when his driver needed surgery. As a gesture of kindness towards their colleague, none of the doctors nor the surgeon who performed the surgery charged any fees. But the hospital charged its regulation ₹2.2 lakh for OT and equipment usage. The doctor was outraged but the hospital was adamant. So, while none of the doctors earned any money for the treatment, the hospital profited from the driver – who earns only about ₹25,000 per month.

Dual dilemma

South Asia has a unique contradiction of on one hand, being an affordable healthcare destination for those from developed nations – with private hospitals boasting the latest diagnostic and surgical equipment and performing some of the highest numbers of complicated surgeries (such as liver transplants) in the world – while on the other, being unable to offer large swathes of its own population access to lifesaving surgery or even quality healthcare. This was highlighted in a 2017 article by Dr Sanjay Nagral and Dr Samiran Nundy, titled 'Unmet Need for Surgery in South Asia'.[5]

The authors have been vocal about various aspects of medical ethics. In their article, they write that changing cultures and lifestyles have led to a considerable growth in demand for cosmetic, bariatric and arthroscopic surgeries. In the absence of regulations, hospitals have actively worked towards increasing demand, leading to a rise in the number of 'unnecessary procedures'. 'For example, a cross-sectional analysis of data from Bangladesh, India and Nepal showed higher rates of caesarean section in private healthcare facilities than in public ones, even when adjusted for pregnancy, delivery, maternal characteristics and year of delivery,' the authors note in their article. This uncontrolled growth, they say, is largely driven by market forces deepening the existing inequities in surgical care availability in this part of the world.

The article also mentions that advanced surgeries – such as procedures for the treatment of cancer, organ transplants and functional brain surgery – are now available in the region and offer hope to those diagnosed with diseases that until recently had very poor prognosis. This has, however, increased healthcare costs substantially as most patients are uninsured and unable to afford the cost of these treatments. The authors rue the lack of impetus to analyse the cost effectiveness of these complex surgical procedures that can cause grave financial hardships to families.

One of India's best-known gastroenterologists, Dr Nundy would be a familiar face to those who used to watch the television programme *The World This Week*, where he would discuss health issues with the host, Prannoy Roy. He and Dr Nagral have also coedited the book *Healers or Predators: Healthcare Corruption in India*, which was published by Oxford University Press in 2018. It is a sharp and insightful take on the ills plaguing Indian healthcare, many of which hinge on decisions taken by doctors. Vinay Kumaran, a transplant surgeon, contributes an essay to the book, writing about a metric called 'billing per day per bed'. He describes it as the most important metric for administrators at hospitals and explains it using a comparison between the per-day billing for a patient admitted for an elective surgery (about ₹10,000) and that of an organ transplant patient (which could reach an average of ₹1,00,000). While the performance of an organ transplant programme is limited by the number of people willing to donate, that is not the case with many elective surgeries.

For the rich, money is not a constraint, and they willingly undergo expensive surgeries for weight loss or for cosmetic purposes. At the other extreme are those who line the pavements outside AIIMS in the Delhi chill, too poor to be able to afford a place to stay and with no access to the same quality of healthcare in their hometowns. They struggle to travel for treatment to bigger cities. One of the steps taken to change that situation was the opening of AIIMS across the country. Unfortunately, merely conferring the revered acronym is yet to guarantee the same excellence of services in the 22 institutions (apart from the original in Delhi) that currently exist in the country. Another step towards improving healthcare affordability was the rollout of the Pradhan Mantri Jan Arogya Yojana – the tertiary care arm of the NDA government's flagship health programme Ayushman Bharat – under which eligible families are entitled to an annual health cover of ₹5 lakh.

However, empanelment of hospitals under PMJAY has been slow, with a little over 14,000 of the 43,000-odd private hospitals in the country choosing to enrol.[6] Hospitals say that the ceiling rates under the programme are too low for them to break even. Yet, in some smaller centres, the programme has resulted in an unlikely boost in business for private setups and created inflationary pressure, as per public health researcher Dr Shailendra Hooda, who is an associate professor at the Institute for Studies in Industrial Development.

Dr Hooda and his team have tracked the cost of healthcare in Rajasthan from the time when the only health insurance available to the poor was the RSBY. The annual cover provided under RSBY was ₹30,000. In 2015, the state government launched the Bhamashah Swasthya Bima Yojana and subsumed RSBY into it. This took the total health coverage to ₹3,30,000, with a distinction being made between general (limit of ₹30,000) and serious (cover of ₹3,00,000) illnesses.[7] Then came PMJAY in 2018, and the annual family health insurance increased significantly.

Dr Hooda explains, 'For each of these insurance programmes, there was a rate list for hospitals. For example, under RSBY the rate for a natural childbirth ranged from ₹2,500 to ₹4,500. But the hospital had to spend ₹3,000 to ₹3,500 for each procedure, so they would sometimes ask patients to pay the difference. They mostly agreed. Under Bhamashah, the rate was revised to about ₹5,000, which led to a comfortable balance and the hospitals made a small profit. Under PMJAY, the rates went up to ₹9,000.' As a precaution against unnecessary procedures, PMJAY mandates that caesarean sections and high-risk deliveries can be done in private hospitals only if there is a referral from a government centre. Regular deliveries face no such restrictions.

'But what also happened is that this ₹9,000 became the benchmark,' says Dr Hooda. 'Hospitals started saying that this is the fixed rate for the procedure and you must pay this amount, insurance or no insurance. So, while 40 per cent of the population is covered under PMJAY, for the others – except for the miniscule percentage with the ability to pay for private insurance – there was in effect an increase in medical expenditure after PMJAY was implemented.' While Dr Hooda's assessment on the inflationary impact of PMJAY will need some scrutiny, there are other existing structural issues in the government health insurance schemes that sometimes make them counterproductive. One such issue is the pendency of dues.

According to NHA – which implements PMJAY and now also oversees disbursement for other government insurance schemes – as of 18 February 2025, a total of ₹1,095 crore worth of bills are yet to be disbursed by the CGHS.[8] These are bills that have been rigorously scrutinised and vetted by the NHA before being sent to the CGHS. Unfortunately, the latter remains an organisation notorious for its inertia. This pendency has been flagged numerous times by private hospital associations but not much has changed.

The other problem is the wide variation in the approved rates for health insurance schemes run by the Centre and various state governments.

Asking to remain anonymous, a senior surgeon who works at a prominent private hospital in Kolkata told me that all of these rates are usually significantly lower than what it costs the hospital for various surgeries. For example, in West Bengal, the rates of the state government's health insurance programme, called Swasthya Sathi, are different from that of PMJAY, which in turn are different from the General Insurance Public Sector Association (GIPSA) rates. Then there is the CGHS, which too has its own rates. The surgeon gives an example of the procedure for the removal of uretic stones. At the hospital where he works, the total cost would amount to about ₹65,000. But the CGHS rate for that surgery is set at ₹19,300.

'How does the hospital meet the difference?' the surgeon asks. 'Should it recover the outstanding amount from other patients by whatever means possible? What we do is we split one surgery into multiple procedures. So instead of just billing for a stone removal, we bill for every step – cystoscopy, insertion of the guide wire, ureteroscopy, the actual breaking of the stones and stenting. Each is billed as a separate procedure.' He admits that if they were to do it for private insurance companies, the bills would never get cleared.

'But the scrutiny is relatively lax for the CGHS,' he reveals. 'Our cashiers know that, so when there is a CGHS patient the bills are automatically structured like this. Even if there is scrutiny, the hospital does not really care. The worst that can happen is that we are de-empanelled. Given the low rates of the CGHS, that is something many hospitals want. So, these billing practices are really a win-win proposition for them. They either make some profits or they get thrown out of a scheme they don't want to be a part of anyway.'

Sleights and subterfuge

In 2023, Bloomberg blew the lid off what it called a 'scandal' in the USA. The report revealed that senior surgeons were billing insurance companies for procedures that they did not perform themselves. The surgeries were done by others in their team, usually the surgical residents.[9] However, in India, this is such a common practice that it is not even talked about. This is despite some Indian surgeons claiming to perform incredible numbers of surgeries every week.

A prominent cardiac surgeon in the country was at one point reputed to be doing about 20 surgeries a week, each taking an average of four hours to complete. That comes to about 14 hours per day in surgery. The surgeon in question is also a regular at prominent social events. How does he do it? 'Very simple – he doesn't,' says one of his colleagues. 'His team does the surgeries. He is present in the OTs during some of the operations, but it is not humanly possible to have those kinds of hours. However, he is the one who builds the relationship with patients who trust him.'

The main surgeon answers any queries the patients may have and convinces them that what he will do on the operation table is their best shot at healing. However, a carefully recruited set of very good doctors are the ones actually performing the surgeries. 'So we cannot say that that doctor has done a few thousand open-heart surgeries, when it really is a team effort,' declares the colleague of the famous cardiac surgeon. That cardiac surgeon is not alone. Many other senior surgeons across disciplines have teams that execute various parts of the procedure or, sometimes, the entire procedure.

Given the volume of patients that Indian hospitals handle, it is simply not feasible for one surgeon to single-handedly do all the surgeries that are billed in their name. Journalist Asha Dubey found this out the hard way when she was detected with a lump in her breast. She went to an oncologist in a corporate hospital that she knew and trusted. The doctor told her that the lump needed to be removed but asked her not to worry as he would 'handle' it personally. Asha was sent for some very expensive tests and then asked to return to the hospital at 6 a.m. on the appointed day.

'The doctor told me that I would be able to go home by 8 a.m.,' she recounts. However, when she reached the hospital as asked, accompanied by her son, there was nobody around, not even the doctor who had promised to 'take care' of her. It was a scary experience. Finally, it was at around 8.30 a.m. that the first staff started trickling in. Even when she was wheeled into the surgery for cauterisation (burning of tissue), her doctor was nowhere to be seen. 'I had chosen to do it under local anaesthesia,' she reveals. 'It was quite painful, but at least I could see who was performing the surgery. My doctor was still absent. When I asked the other doctors where he was, they told me that he would not be coming in that day as he was busy somewhere else.'

Asha says that she felt cheated. She went home at 4 p.m. the same day and was billed ₹1.90 lakh for the short procedure. 'When I went back to the doctor and asked him why he was not there, he told me that the doctor who did the surgery is "very good" and that he had "trained" him himself,' says Asha. 'I could not ask him what that doctor's surgery fee was, but it was probably different from his own, which is what I had been billed for.' Had she been under general anaesthesia, she might not have ever known who performed the procedure. The biopsy came clean and the doctor asked her to do more tests just 'to be sure'. She never went back for them.

For a hospital, the 'star' doctor (such as the one Asha consulted) is the proverbial golden goose. It is their name that attracts patients to that particular hospital, willing to pay a premium to be treated by that doctor. However, like Asha, they often find out later that the doctor would not actually be present during their surgery. Logistically speaking, this is inevitable because Indian hospitals in both government and private sectors handle patient volumes that are so high that a reputed doctor's hands are always full and they need a team to assist them. But for patients it can still feel like betrayal. In fact, some of the best known institutes in developed nations do not handle even a fraction of the patient load of big Indian hospitals.

A liver transplant surgeon wanted to train abroad after a few years of practice in India. During the admissions process for the fellowship, he was asked in the interview about the number of transplants his centre did. 'When I told them we do about 200 to 250 per year, they responded by saying that then I should train them instead because they do only a quarter of that number annually,' he says. However, he points out that though most transplant centres in India have a single transplant surgeon in whose name that unit runs, it is not possible for that one person to do all the required surgeries. 'All transplants require two surgeries,' he reminds me. 'One for the recipient, one for the donor. Naturally it is very important to have a good support team.'

While this business model rakes in revenue, hospitals are also wary of being too dependent on one name and losing out on most of their business should that one doctor leave and join the competitor. That is why many hospitals have now started relying more on a marketing strategy that establishes their own name as the brand rather than boast about having a particular doctor like they used to. However, patients continue to put a lot of faith in individual surgeons. That is why some of them notch up bigger surgery numbers than others.

There are now many surgeries that can be done without a hospital stay. However, not being admitted to hospital often doesn't mean that the bill would be any less harsh on the patient's pocket. Sanjay, a busy corporate executive, had been suffering from back pain for a while but had been putting off the minor procedure his doctor had recommended as he did not want to stay in hospital. But when the pain got unbearable, and his doctor mentioned the word 'cancer', his resolve began to be tested. But the clincher for him was when he was told that he would not need to be admitted. The surgery was only a day procedure, and he could just take half a day off from work to get it done.

Sanjay arrived at the hospital at 8 a.m. on the appointed day, after assuring his office that he would be back at his desk by 3 p.m. The first hiccup he encountered was when he was told that his doctor had been called away for an emergency surgery and would not be able to begin his procedure scheduled for 9 a.m. Then, by the time his doctor was available, the OT was no longer free. Eventually, the surgery was only completed at 4 p.m., and he could not leave until 6 p.m.

His insurance paid for the procedure so he did not pay much attention to the bill. It was therefore much later that Sanjay realised that he had been billed for bed charges of ₹1,800 per hour for 10 hours. He had paid ₹18,000 for the day use of the bed, when the tariff for a single room for an overnight stay was ₹6,500 plus GST. There is a 5 per cent GST on non-ICU hospital beds that cost more than ₹5,000 per day. The bed charges were in addition to the other costs of the procedure, such as OT charges and the surgeon's fee.

A resident doctor in the ophthalmology department of a corporate hospital tells me that the unexpected truth is very few surgeries become cheaper by opting for day procedures over being admitted for a night. 'Patients have various reasons for opting for day procedures,' he says, 'but the expectation always is that it will be cheaper. When they get the bill, they are in for a nasty surprise.' He warns that the larger private hospitals have become adept at ensuring all bills are paid in full before a patient leaves the hospital, including those that have been contested.

Such is the randomness of the billing practices of private hospitals that the dues may go up by almost a quarter of the original bill if a patient chooses to switch from claiming insurance to paying out of pocket. Sunil Kumar had been admitted to a private hospital in Gurgaon with some minor complaints such as diarrhoea and dehydration He stayed in a twin sharing room and was handed a bill of ₹59,309 at the time of discharge.[10] The bill was sent to his insurance company, which took a long time to approve it. Sunil couldn't leave the hospital until it was paid, so he decided to pay himself and go home instead of waiting around. He planned to claim reimbursement later from the insurance provider.

But the hospital told him that if he didn't use his insurance, the bill would change to ₹75,377 – an increase of 27 per cent. Most of the extra amount was being charged for 'consultation' and 'other procedures', leaving Sunil stumped. The reason for the difference is that hospitals have contracts with individual insurance companies that specify the rates that they can charge. This means that in effect insurance companies have become something of a rudimentary regulator of healthcare costs, a role that rightfully and obligatorily should belong to the government. But when a patient pays out of pocket, that contractual obligation no longer exists and the hospital can charge as they please, leaving patients at their mercy. But hospital executives say that this is nothing more than standard billing procedure. Sunil's hospital too claimed that it was an 'industry-wide practice' when asked to respond on the matter.

It is well known that hospitals refuse to release patients unless bills have been paid. What is not as widely known is that sometimes hospitals will start harassing their own staff for unpaid bills. A senior journalist found out about this when his mother was hospitalised in an emergency. 'She had several chronic conditions and was being treated as an outpatient at the hospital for a long time,' he explained. 'But when she developed complications, I approached the person in charge of media relations to ensure that my mother was admitted as soon as possible. The media relations executive was very helpful and helped me secure a bed for my mother.'

During the long hospitalisation period, the journalist began to get calls from the billing department of the hospital. Soon, the office of the medical superintendent also called and asked him to pay at least a part of the bill. 'I was very distressed, and I told them that my mother was with them, so I couldn't run away without paying,' he said. 'I promised to pay them and asked them to concentrate on her treatment.' But the calls continued, and he had to tell them that it now amounted to harassment. 'It was only after my mother passed away that I found out that the media relations executive who had helped me had also started receiving calls from her colleagues in the billing department, who were threatening her that the money would be deducted from her salary if I did not pay up,' reveals the journalist.

As the incidents in this chapter illustrate, many doctors and staff members at corporate hospitals are conscious of the power they have of doing good, and they occasionally choose to exercise it, sometimes at their own peril. But the well-oiled hospital machinery geared towards making maximum profit often overpowers any individual's attempts to ease a patient's financial burden.

3

The 'Package' Deal

During the COVID-19 pandemic, the central government fixed the maximum per-day package rates that private hospitals could charge patients suffering from the viral infection. It took a pandemic, a declaration of public health emergency and an intervention from the home minister for ceiling rates to be fixed in 2020 for 60 per cent of COVID-19 isolation beds.[1] These rates also included medicines, which significantly changed the normal pricing dynamics of private hospitals. The government choosing to regulate rates during a dire public health situation shows that it is aware that hospital charges in the private sector are a problem. It also demonstrated that, contrary to its usual stance, the government has both the mandate and the means to control healthcare costs. It is perhaps just not on the list of priorities either of the central government or the state governments.

Unfortunately for India's large population of uninsured people, government checks on hospital rates disappeared as soon as the immediate urgency of the pandemic waned. This, even after the need for such regulation has been highlighted many times in multiple conversations and litigations. A promising start was made with the Clinical Establishments Act in 2010, but it failed to make the kind of impact it had the potential for because of lack of follow-through. Even for a packet of biscuits, the law mandates that the manufacturers print MRP on the wrapper. But when it comes to private hospitals and nursing homes, information about healthcare costs in the form of a rate chart can often be difficult to get. In corporate hospitals, it is almost impossible. Hospitals occasionally display room rates like a hotel does but do not usually put details about the actual cost of treatment. It is possible to view this as an unfair trade practice, because the service that a hospital provides, unlike a hotel, is not a room to sleep in but the treatment of an ailment. The actual cost of that service is shrouded in opacity.

In the case of preventive health packages, however, the price is often the sales pitch for the service. There are numerous packages that include a certain number of tests for a fixed, discounted price. But the hospital often uses the results of these tests to steer patients towards more tests and consultations based on real or extrapolated conclusions and perceived risks. Therein lies their true value.

Media professional Lata Wilson was stunned when she found out about the differences in the price for cancer surgery offered by a corporate hospital in Delhi and a charitable hospital run by a religious organisation in Kottayam. Her mother had been suffering from a stomachache that the family had initially dismissed as gas. When antacids did not make any difference, she was taken to a small hospital near her home in Kerala. When she was diagnosed with advanced colorectal cancer that had also started invading her stomach, the family brought her to Delhi, where her daughter was working.

Lata first went to a prominent cancer surgeon at a corporate hospital in the city, whom she knew in her professional capacity. 'He told me that my mother would need surgery in which many parts of her lower gastrointestinal tract would have to be cut off,' Lata recalls. He gave her the impression that he was offering her a discounted rate, given their long professional association, when quoting an estimate of ₹18 lakh to ₹20 lakh. This price included the cost of surgery, doctors' fees and hospitalisation charges, but the follow-up chemotherapy and radiotherapy would have cost extra.

'My mother had no medical insurance, but we decided that somehow, as a family, we would find the money to give her the best care possible. But she wanted to be near my father in Kerala,' says Lata. As the family was debating this, a friend referred them to a hospital in Kottayam for a second opinion.

They were stunned when doctors there offered to do the same surgery for ₹3 lakh! Lata took her mother to Kottayam, where the surgery happened successfully. After including the costs for the aggressive chemotherapy and radiotherapy that followed, the total bill came to less than ₹10 lakh – about half of what the package cost at the Delhi hospital that did not include the follow-up treatment.

'My mother was very happy, because the doctors at Kottayam were very nice,' Lata shares. 'They called her "amma" and spent a long time talking to her. She now has to live with a colostomy bag attached to her body, but she has adjusted well to it. And the best part for my fiercely independent mother was that she paid for the surgery herself without either my sister or I having to pitch in.'

In most hospitals, even the rates for standard, frequently administered medical procedures are not displayed prominently. As a matter of routine, samples are immediately sent post admission for tests such as blood sugar, urine routine or estimation of total blood count, but their charges can be revealed only at the time of billing. There is no cut-off threshold above which additional charges can be disclosed in advance. There is total opacity.

How much does it cost to put a patient on a catheter, and how much to take them off it? How much does it cost to prick a patient and check their blood sugar? What is the cost of a cannula insertion? The answer can vary depending on hospital, geography or even category of rooms. In some cases the charges may vary from patient to patient in the same hospital. Rates for all standard procedures are linked to the bed rent. The same surgery performed by the same doctor and with the same medicines and consumables can cost more for the patient in a suite room than for the one sharing a room with three others. However, this is rarely explained to the patient at the time of admission though following periodic outcries over the practice, consumer awareness about it has increased in recent years.

A transplant surgeon at a prominent hospital chain in North India confirms this. 'For a patient staying in a single room, the liver transplant package is about ₹2 lakh more than for somebody sharing a room,' he reveals. 'The same rates are given to patients with insurance, but how much their insurance company actually reimburses is a different matter.'

This variation in procedure rates is a result of the government's policy of leaving healthcare to what is commonly called 'market forces', to the fallacious premise that a person looking for treatment for a life-threatening medical condition faces the same choice as a person looking for, say, a packet of biscuits and will therefore reject a product (in this case, healthcare) that they think is not worth the money being demanded for it. The truth is they do not even have the information required to assess the quality of care offered to them. Hospital accreditation stamps such as the one given out by the National Accreditation Board for Hospital and Healthcare Providers (NABH) are not really understood by the average Indian.

Hospitals in smaller cities and towns do not even bother about these. The doctor therefore becomes the axis on which the entire system revolves. As the repository of all information and options, they can channel patient decisions in any direction they want. There is scant scrutiny of the quality of their advice or the motives driving them. The patient has no option but to trust that the doctor is competent, stays abreast of the latest developments in their field and practises ethically. However, there are enough instances available in the public domain (some of which are discussed in this book) that have made this belief increasingly shaky. The financial implications of the 'choice' given to the patient are discussed only if the patient seeks that information: if the patient has a hefty insurance cover or deep pockets, it may not be discussed at all. Most such patients will simply ask, 'How much will it cost me?' but will rarely go into the breakup of those costs once the insurance approvals come through. Detailed estimates are shared with the insurance company before treatment starts, and any escalations beyond a reasonable limit have to be justified by the hospital. For uninsured patients, estimates are shared in a less formal mode, sometimes verbally. Escalations can sometimes be steep and explanations perfunctory, with hospitals not shying away even from strong-arm methods to extract payment. Lack of a written estimate precludes any cost-related accountability of either the doctor or the hospital.

But in a transparent system, a written estimate of treatment costs would be a routine pre-hospitalisation process, irrespective of the insurance status, with no room for fluctuations for more than 10 per cent to 15 per cent. Any potential escalations above this range should be discussed with the patient, ideally before that treatment modality is adopted, instead of presenting a bill at the time of discharge.

In the interest of total transparency, in addition to the doctors' fee, hospitalisation charges and procedure costs, any additional incentives for doctors should also be disclosed right at the start. Insurance companies have devised their own ways of negotiating this randomness in hospital rates. They have contracts with corporate hospitals on the rates that patients they cover would be entitled to. There are other safeguards as well.

For example, the practice of linking procedure costs to room rent is the reason why insurance companies have a cap on room rents. Putting such a limit ensures that there is in effect also a cap on doctors' fees, medication costs and procedure charges, given that all those rates increase with the room rent.

Bhaskar Nerurkar, head of the health administration team at Bajaj Allianz General Insurance, explained the reasons and implications for capping room rent in health insurance plans in an article published in *Deccan Herald* in March 2023, where he explained that if the insured person exceeds the room rent limit specified in the policy, then a concept called 'proportionate deductions' comes into effect.[2] The insurer, at the time of settling the claim, looks at by how much the capped room rent has been exceeded and then makes a proportionate deduction from all 'associated medical expenses'. This is called room rent co-pay.

Nerurkar also wrote that because charges like doctors' fees and operation costs are linked to the room rent, a surgery that costs ₹15,000 in a twin-shared room would be charged ₹20,000 if the patient opts for a private air-conditioned room, while for a higher category accommodation, such as a suite, the same surgery may cost ₹1 lakh.[3] The only exception to this clause of proportionate deduction in insurance is for medicines, as they are sold at MRP. But as already discussed in Chapter 1, most drugs are not under price control, and the listed MRP is a largely unregulated marketing ruse designed to extract profits at every stage of the supply chain from the pocket of the patient.

No room for deviation

Most package rates cover only regular procedures with no scope to accommodate complications or other differences in the physical response of individual patients to treatment. Some patients have a slower rate of recovery and need an extra day in hospital after surgery. In other cases, the patient's pre-operative test may throw up a surprise that needs an extra couple of days before the operation can be done. Those extra days and any additional procedures or treatments that may be needed are then charged separately. Often, patients with pre-existing medical conditions, which may increase the odds of a lengthier recovery period, are immediately declared ineligible for a package.

A senior cardiac surgeon at a posh private hospital in Delhi admits that treatment packages work only for certain patients because they are designed to offer only the minimum level of care and hospitalisation. For example, a package for a coronary artery bypass graft (CABG) – commonly known as a 'bypass surgery' – includes six days of hospitalisation, post-surgery monitoring and stepdown care. But if the patient suffers blood loss during the surgery and needs a transfusion or a sudden drop in his platelet count necessitates a haematologist consultation, neither would be covered by the package. Some of the common complications of

CABG such as limb weakness, vision problems or speech difficulty need a referral to a neurologist. But neither the consultation nor the subsequent management is covered by the package even though a significant number of patients need them.

'In each of these instances, there will be additional billing for doctor consultations, interventions and medications,' the cardiac surgeon elaborates. 'This is never explicitly explained to the patient at the time of admission. Only the risks of the operation are outlined, but the possible cost implications are not. No matter the branch of medicine, in almost every hospital package there are numerous such grey areas that are never disclosed beforehand.'

There is little oversight over how patients are being billed. Sometimes, doctors add packages that may not be in their domain of expertise at all – for example, a surgeon adding a clinical care package in their bill. While such interventions may occasionally be necessary, repeated inclusion of such unusual packages in a doctor's billing should be treated as a red flag, because every such package includes a fixed fee for the doctor. But the internal audit mechanisms that can catch such transgressions barely exist; where they do, they are not looking for overbilling-related issues. For a patient with no knowledge of medicine or the ways of corporate hospitals, it is impossible to keep track of all the tests done during hospitalisation or scrutinise the final bill to check if any extra items have been added. Medical jargon can also be intimidating – few patients can distinguish between a test for C-reactive protein (CRP) which is a marker for inflammation and Complete Blood Count (CBC) which takes stock of the numbers of various blood cells to assess whether there is inflammation or infection. That is why even the most diligent patients who are in the habit of checking invoices closely may not be able to easily spot discrepancies in a medical bill.

However, sometimes the extra item on the bill is so blatant that it stands out even to a layman. Nikhil Sen, a photographer, was one such patient. He had been admitted to a prominent private hospital in East Delhi with acute pancreatitis. Discharged after three days, he found that along with all the other charges, he had also been billed for a urine test. 'Even in my dazed, tired state I knew that at no point in time had I given a urine sample,' claims Nikhil. 'The nurses had drawn blood several times. There were several blood reports though I had no energy to match the reports against the tests mentioned on the bill, but they could not have done a urine test because they never had a sample.'

When he flagged the issue, a manager told him that the test was essential, and if it hadn't been done, he could give a sample right there and the test would be done. 'But why should I do a test that is not needed for my treatment? Just because the insurance will pay for it? I refused,' Nikhil says. The manager too stuck to his guns, but after a few calls to the public relations department of the hospital, the charge for the urine test was reversed. Nikhil was lucky because the discrepancy between samples collected and tests billed was immediately obvious. Since his hospital stay was short, the bill was also only a few pages that could be easily checked. But after a long hospitalisation, a hospital invoice can run to several pages. In those cases, last-minute additions to the bill are difficult to verify.

Imagine a situation where a patient was admitted in an emergency and has undergone an angioplasty. An angioplasty is a minimally invasive procedure in which blockages in blood vessels are removed. This is done with a balloon that pushes the offending clot out or by using a stent. A stent is a tiny mesh tube inserted into a weak vessel to make it more resilient. The cost of an angioplasty package changes depending on the type and the number of stents used for the procedure. A patient has no option but to take the doctor's word on the type and number of stents used. That was the experience of a senior government officer when a family member was taken ill. 'It was a Saturday, and I was home in Gandhinagar when my father complained of heartburn. We rushed him to the family physician's clinic. He did an ECG and asked us to immediately take him to hospital. When we reached there we were told that he would have to be taken for an emergency angioplasty.'

The doctor also told the family that there are many varieties of stents, some manufactured indigenously and some imported. A German import was advised as the best option in his case. 'At that point we were scared and confused. What did we know or understand about these things? We just said that we want the very best for him. They inserted three stents that day and one more the next day,' the officer recalls. This was before stents had been brought under price control, so the family ended up paying a few lakh rupees out of pocket despite having some government insurance coverage. Years later, when the old gentleman suffered heart failure and was taken to AIIMS in Delhi, the family learned that inserting four stents at one time was 'very unusual'. Despite this, when he returned to the hospital in his hometown following the AIIMS stint, another three stents were put in.

It is common practice for hospitals to push for an 'emergency' angioplasty after a routine or elective angiogram – an imaging technique that is used to check the health of blood vessels. This is never warranted, according to top cardiac specialists.[4] In some situations, doctors advocate stent use in patients with 50 per cent or 60 per cent blockage, even though it is not advisable for those with less than 90 per cent blockage. Unnecessary angioplasties can lead to complications such as restenosis, in which a thinned blood vessel that has been fixed narrows once again and causes an impediment to the smooth flow of blood. The patient also runs the risk of excessive bleeding even from small injuries because of blood thinners that they must take for life.

Overuse of stents is one of the better documented examples of overtreatment in India. Studies have indicated that stenting is only as effective as medical therapy and sometimes less so. In one review that was published in *JAMA Internal Medicine* in 2012, the researchers concluded that initial stenting for stable coronary artery disease shows no apparent benefit compared with early administration of drugs for prevention of death or complications such as myocardial infarction, or angina.[5] CAD refers to coronary artery disease. Coronary artery is the blood vessel that supplies the heart muscle with blood. Any blockage in it can affect the efficiency of the heart's pumping action. MI or myocardial infarction refers to what we commonly refer to as heart attack. Angina is the pain that is associated with constricted blood supply to the heart muscle. There are many such studies published in globally reputed journals, yet Indian surgeons' preference for stents continues. In 2017, some of the biggest names in the field came out and said that one in every three stents implanted in Indian patients were probably not necessary.[6]

Patients are easily swayed by doctors' recommendations, so they might choose a more expensive option even if they can't afford it only because the doctor says it is 'better' for them. That is how information bias directs choices. Lawyer Ashok Aggarwal's work in helping poor patients access private healthcare, which they are entitled to under various agreements between Delhi government and private hospitals, has been mentioned earlier in this book. He tells me about the travails of one of his clients, who had been admitted with heart blockage under the non-paying patients' quota at a big private hospital. The doctor told him that since he was a non-paying patient, he would only get the stent costing ₹30,000 and not the medically appropriate stent costing ₹1.5 lakh unless he was willing to pay the balance out of pocket. The patient was in a bind, because he did not want to compromise on his treatment but could not afford the expensive option either. This is the kind of Hobson's Choice that patients are frequently required to negotiate when they access private healthcare.

This incident was from the time when drug-eluting stents (DES) were popular and prices had gone through the roof because there was no regulation. It was common to find stents priced at a few lakh rupees each and there were recurrent complaints of overtreatment and overcharging. It forced the National Pharmaceutical Pricing Authority (NPPA) to step in with price regulations. Now, despite criticism and opposition from the industry, the price of stents is controlled using the same formula that is applied to essential medicines. The latest revision in May 2024 fixed the price of bare metal stents at ₹10,509 per unit and DES at ₹38,267 per unit.[7]

Preventive packages

Preventive health check-up packages are a money-spinner for hospitals, not in terms of direct revenue but definitely for their additional revenue generation potential. The rising numbers of gallbladder and kidney stone removals are often linked to the popularity of preventive health checks. Gallbladder stones are very common and rarely require intervention unless the patient has symptoms. Nestled in the folds of the intestine and sandwiched between the liver and the pancreas, the gallbladder is a tiny organ that stores a substance called bile. Bile is first secreted by the liver from which it travels to the gallbladder through the bile ducts. In the gallbladder, bile stays and keeps getting increasingly concentrated. It is finally released when a meal is consumed, particularly when it contains fat. Bile helps in the digestion and absorption of fat. What are known as gallbladder stones are pieces of cholesterol (a kind of fat) or of bilirubin (which is a breakdown product of blood cells and is excreted through the bile). Gallbladder stones may vary in size, number and in the symptoms they cause in people. Some may be painful.

Kidney stones, on the other hand are deposits of various minerals that may form inside the kidneys. This may be caused by medications, lack of adequate water intake or even because of excessive body weight. Kidney stones too can be painful but don't always need aggressive measures such as surgical removal.

Before the advent of preventive health tests, many people would live with gallbladder stones or kidney stones without even knowing they had them. But now, the routine ultrasound which is included in a preventive care package easily identifies asymptomatic kidney or gallstones. What follows, especially for insured patients, is a recommendation of surgical removal.

However, medical guidance is to decide on surgical option based on factors such as location and composition of the stones, but most importantly on whether or not the patient is showing any symptoms of discomfort. Despite this, even uninsured, asymptomatic patients are often convinced by their doctors to opt for the surgery on the grounds of long-term health and wellness. A senior gastrointestinal surgeon from Mumbai admits that gallbladder removal because of an incidental finding of stones may be the most frequently abused gastrointestinal surgical procedure. 'In urology that position may belong to kidney stones,' he says.

This surgeon is known for his robust stance and extensive scholarship on the practice of ethical medicine. He holds that the business model of private hospitals – where there may be monetary incentives for surgeons to push unnecessary surgeries or doctors may have 'targets' to meet that make them push patients towards more expensive treatment options – is the real culprit. 'When doctors succumb to these business strategies, the casualty is evidence-based medicine,' he says. 'Doctors also have an inherent tendency to lead the patient towards their own area of specialisation. For example, surgeons will prescribe surgery much more than clinicians. But the defence that excessive surgeries are done to protect medical professionals from litigation is absolute nonsense. I can very emphatically say that I have never practised defensive medicine in my life and no patient has ever taken me to court. There is still a way for doctors to practise their craft ethically but many who do not or cannot do so, hide behind such excuses. The key is transparency and clear communication about the reasons and evidence on which a doctor bases their recommendations.'

Ultrasounds are a non-invasive and relatively safe imaging technology showing the movement of the internal organs of the body in real time. But they also happen to be potent tools of overdiagnosis and overtreatment of conditions such as uterine fibroids, malaria and thyroid problems, and in the hands of an unethical practitioner, also the tool to detect the sex of an unborn child. The last is illegal in India, but the still dipping sex ratios (at birth) of many states is evidence of how rampant that violation (followed by female foeticide) is in the country. Prosecutions of errant doctors are few and far between. Overdiagnosis exposes a patient to the vagaries of the private healthcare system. Although overuse of imaging technologies such as ultrasound to then overtreat is a global phenomenon; India's low public spending on health and abysmal penetration of health insurance make this a far more complex problem than in more developed countries.

The futility of indiscriminate preventive health tests is acknowledged in medical literature. In 2016, the *National Medical Journal of India* published a review in which doctors from several hospitals in Mumbai and Madhya Pradesh concluded that 'routine health check-ups as practised in urban India are counterproductive within the framework of community healthcare'.[8] They questioned the rationale of doing tests for vitamin D, vitamin B12, thyroid-stimulating hormone, electrolytes and pulmonary function without any effort to screen patients beforehand. Instead of offering these tests to those who most needed them, hospitals do tests on whoever wants them and can afford to pay for them, they pointed out.

The consequences of this are overdiagnosis, overtreatment, anxiety because of false positives or complacency over false negatives. There is also the matter of the cost. Unnecessary tests and consequent unnecessary clinical or surgical interventions can result in an enormous expenditure for the patient. For example, a battery of additional tests may be needed to rule out a 'suspicion' of cancer in an otherwise asymptomatic patient who may have turned up for a routine pre-employment health check-up. Even if the basic health check-up is paid for by the employer, the costs for these extra tests and treatments must be borne by the patient. The health packages can come in many shapes and sizes. In this study, the authors noted that the cost ranged from ₹1,650 for a 'mini' health check-up to ₹59,500 for a 'deluxe' package.

There is a school of thought that a multidisciplinary approach can protect patients against the vested interests of an individual doctor who may want to steer them towards a choice that would be profitable for them. On paper, it appears to be a sound strategy but in the complex world of private healthcare, this again turns out to be another ruse to increase hospital bills. Every specialist involved in the care of a patient comes with their own fee and over a longer period of hospitalisation, it can add up to a substantial sum of money.

This has led to an element of quid pro quo creeping into the business in the form of 'referrals'. Doctor A will refer a patient to Doctor B, who will return the favour when a suitable opportunity arises in the future. There are also many stories of doctors choosing to overlook another doctor's transgressions in the hope that their own dubious practices will be similarly overlooked when questions are raised. That is why it is often difficult to get doctors to give evidence against each other even in the gravest of cases of medical negligence and maltreatment. A doctor, in fact, will rarely tell a patient in clear terms that a fellow professional erred even in the privacy of their own clinic.

There are undoubtedly many private hospitals that operate ethically and transparently, and doctors who remain true only to the interest of their patients. But the latter, when they find themselves in an establishment that is not scrupulous, often don't have the power to fight the system. Their only options are capitulation or exit. The cost and duration of a medical education and the changing contours of the financial relationship between doctors and hospitals make it increasingly difficult for doctors to treat patients outside of the hospital system. Even in smaller cities, only the most senior doctors with established practices can thrive without any hospital affiliations.

4

The Hidden Costs

George Mathew, an HR professional, was admitted to a hospital with an acute stomachache. The establishment where he spent three days is part of a big hospital chain with significant presence across North India. Post hospitalisation, he was handed a bill of over ₹75,000, of which ₹4,101 – about 5 per cent – was listed as 'other charges'. The document is a classic example of the myriad and often mysterious ways that hospital bills bulk up. These miscellaneous costs included admission charges, medical evaluation for the third-party administrator (TPA) and medical history assessment. He was also billed thrice for care, hygiene and infection control, one for each day spent in the hospital. The consultant fees made up a few pages of the invoice with a few more listing out the consumables such as syringes, gloves, infusion sets and wet absorption sheets that had been used. These charges were in addition to the bed charges of about ₹5,000 per day for a twin sharing room. It is interesting to note that the bed charges do not automatically include charges for infection control or the basic care the patient receives, despite it being a bed in a hospital and not a hotel. Equally interesting is the fact that medical history assessment was separately invoiced when it would have been done by doctors whose fees were already accounted for.

In 2020, the Insurance Regulatory and Development Authority of India (IRDAI) attempted to bring a modicum of order into the billing processes of corporate hospitals with a master circular for health insurance TPAs (third-party administrators).[1] The circular noted that billing could only happen on some specific heads such as bed and nursing charges, ICU charges, OT charges, medicine and consumables, professional fees, investigation charges, package charges and miscellaneous charges. For each of these, there were also given detailed breakups of the inclusions. However, four years on, hospitals have introduced categories such as 'disinfection fees' and 'additional procedure charges' to sidestep extant regulations. This practice has been identified as one of the contributors to healthcare inflation.[2]

In George's case, doctors classified him as 'NBM' (which stands for 'nothing by mouth'), as he was unable to digest food. Only on the last day, to test whether he was capable of ingesting something without the excruciating pain making a comeback, he was given a small, semi solid meal. So his bill had no charges for meals and consultations with a dietician – two categories that can be found in most hospital bills today. A medicine resident who works at a top hospital explains that earlier hospital food was a simple affair and almost all patients would get the same meal. 'But now all hospitals have a dietician who will visit the patient, ask a few questions about their food preferences and bowel movements and then make individualised recommendations for their food,' he says. 'However, the truth is that not all patients need specialised or even a personalised diet.' The dietician's daily charge might seem small, but in the case of a long hospital stay, it can add up to form a big chunk of the bill. In most cases, insurance covers only a portion of these additional charges.

Hospitals also charge patients for oxygen in the ICU, which was never billed separately until the second wave of COVID-19 hit and oxygen, for the first time ever, became a scarce commodity nationally. India's enterprising healthcare behemoths were quick to pounce on a pandemic-triggered panic to turn oxygen into another source of profit. Despite already levying a Goods and Service Tax (GST) of 2.5 per cent on room rent, hospitals often add an additional 'service charge' to the bill, emulating a controversial practice of the restaurant industry that may have finally been buried following a ruling of the Delhi High Court disallowing it.

Hospitals continue to get away with it. A hospital executive based in Noida admits that the room rents are exorbitant at the hospital where they work while also involving significant exclusions. They do not include the cost of the patient's food, dietician fee or oxygen; even the towel used for sponging the patient and the toiletries provided are separately charged in some cases. 'Sometimes attendants will bluntly tell you that your room rent may be listed as ₹12,000 but in effect is actually ₹20,000,' the executive said.

'Everything is digital these days. Every time a patient is admitted, we charge them ₹7,500 to ₹8,000 for medical records. Honestly, this cannot be a recurring charge; it should be charged only once for a patient, or at least there should be a fixed validity period, maybe a year. If a patient is admitted more than once in the span of a few months, they would be charged each time for medical records, which is not fair,' added the hospital official. 'There is also an "administrative charge" of ₹2,500 that is added to the bill daily. That's an additional ₹25,000 for a ten-day hospitalisation.'

Except during the recent pandemic, the central government has never regulated hospital pricing, choosing instead to hide behind the convenient fact that public health is for state governments to address. In 2019, the minister of state for health and family welfare, Anupriya Patel, told the Lok Sabha that taking corrective measures regarding inflated bills of insured patients falls under the jurisdiction of the state and union territory governments.[3]

She added that the Insurance Regulatory and Development Authority of India (IRDAI), requires all TPAs and insurers to display the agreed rates of health services to policyholders. This is specified as part of an agreement amongst insurers, network providers and TPAs. 'It is further specified that the insurers and TPAs should put in place measures for passing to the policyholders the benefit of any discounts received from hospitals,' said the minister. This is one of countless such answers that have been given in both Houses of Parliament by successive governments. Patel also told the House that these norms are expected to promote fair practices by hospitals and enhance transparency.[4]

This reluctance to seek accountability from the private sector has far reaching consequences. In 2023, insurance technology company Plum Insurance released a report titled 'Health Report of Corporate India'.[5] The report estimates that at an annual growth of 14 per cent, healthcare inflation in India is the highest in Asia. It highlights that the average cost of consulting a general physician is ₹300 while for a specialist it becomes ₹1,000. The sum further increases to ₹2,500 to consult a mental health professional. Corporate employees, who make up a small part of the Indian population, annually spend ₹12,000 to ₹48,000 on medications with an average spend of ₹1,500 on a health check-up, while for laboratory tests the cost is around ₹25,000 on an average.

While the report did not mention the geographical disparities, it is well known that consultation charges of specialists can vary widely based on location. Gurgaon resident Aditi Sinha discovered this when her husband contracted COVID-19 and suffered such severe lung damage that he was forced to move out of Delhi NCR. 'The pulmonologist in Goa who diagnosed his condition charged ₹500 per visit,' she says. 'But the doctor at the corporate hospital we went to in Delhi – who did not even do a chest X-ray to find out what was causing his discomfort – charged ₹3,000.'

Medical literature is largely silent on the billing practices of private hospitals, but hospital bills reveal many ways in which Indians pay extra for private healthcare. While inflation in healthcare does have a strong correlation to the living expenses of a city, excess charges are not limited to Tier I cities; they exist wherever branches of well-known hospital chains exist. These hidden charges remain constant, no matter what the diagnosis or the treatment. Yet, the intrinsic faith that most Indians still have in doctors ensures that medical bills are not scrutinised enough, so long as they are not beyond the means of the patient. Even the more sceptical ones may find it difficult to make much sense of hospital bills, thwarted by the rampant use of abbreviations and medical jargon. But every once in a while, when families gather the courage and conviction to challenge random charges, they can be waived off. Corporate hospitals are usually eager to avoid anything that might lead to a public relations disaster, so threatening to publicise a dispute using traditional media or social media can sometimes resolve matters in the patient's favour.

Publishing professional Prerna Dwivedi tells me about the time her grandmother had a fall at home. 'My father rushed her to a big hospital chain in Gwalior, where they said that by law they would have to file a medicolegal case (MLC),' she recalls. 'We agreed. But when the bill came, we found a charge of ₹2,500 for the MLC. If this is a procedure that the hospital has to carry out as per government regulations – which is what they had told us – why were we being asked to pay? We threatened to go public with the issue, which is when they finally took it off our bill.' Prerna says that she has since then heard of many such cases in Gwalior. 'We do not even know what the legal position is and what kinds of medical cases MLCs are mandatory for. Do those provisions mandate that the patient should be charged for the paperwork?' she complains. 'Are they really needed? We did not see any documentation so if they had really completed the paperwork, we could not verify it. Without that why would we agree to pay the money?'

Various states have different levels of redress available for patients who feel neglected or fleeced by hospitals. For example, in West Bengal, the government set up the West Bengal Clinical Establishment Regulatory Commission in 2017 to handle such complaints. The commission finds that cases of medical negligence are often beyond its remit, but it does follow up complaints of overcharging. In one such complaint (INT/KOL/2022/198) which was filed by Suman Roy against Lifeline Diagnostic Centre cum Nursing Home, the order exposes the systemic gaps that lead to healthcare inflation.[6] A patient was admitted on 1 May 2021 at 11.40 p.m. and passed away the following day at 3.30 p.m. Despite being in hospital for less than 24 hours, the patient had been charged for two days. There were also unreasonable charges for doctor consultations. The commission found the nursing home guilty of inflated billing and directed it to reduce the bill by ₹9,000. It also ruled that there is no scope for service charge and reversed the ₹18,000 billed under that head, ordered a refund for discounted medicines and consumables and also directed that the money billed as fees for the visits of the resident medical officer (RMO) be returned to the patient. It argued that any patient admitted to a medical establishment is entitled to free RMO service. It also closely scrutinised the fees of the other doctors charged and ordered some deductions. RMOs function at the cusp of clinical disciplines and hospital administration; they are qualified medical practitioners but their job is to look after overall patient services rather than treatment of a single patient.

It is not uncommon for hospitals to charge patients for visits by doctors other than the treating practitioner. Lawyer Ashok Aggarwal says: 'A director at a private hospital once told me during an informal conversation that the billing department has been issued a standing instruction to add one visit by him to the bill of every patient admitted to the 100-bed establishment.' Aggarwal also exposes a very common practice to increase the final bill amount. 'Hospitals often do not discharge patients on a Sunday,' he says. 'This is entirely for the hospital's convenience as many staff members have a day off, but the patients have to pay for an extra day's charges.'

For a long time, Aggarwal has been fighting for the rights of poor patients against Delhi's private hospitals in the hope of making them aware of their right to health so that they understand its importance and start demanding it. That hope has long ebbed, but he recently contested the Delhi Legislative Assembly elections, unsuccessfully.

The fine print

It is not uncommon for patients to find at the time of discharge that the final bill includes charges for tests or visits that never happened or for equipment that was never used but merely kept on standby.

The costs incurred because of compromised medical decision-making are more difficult to identify. Doctors have varying degrees of acceptance about the lack of ethical conduct by fellow professionals in their industry. Some are very open about accepting that all is not well with their profession, particularly after the advent of big pharma and corporate hospital chains – these doctors are the reason this book has been made possible – while others continue to be in denial.

Many doctors I approached chose to decline giving interviews by saying things like 'I have never been asked to increase profits by my hospital,' and dismissing any cited instances of such practices as 'hearsay'. A senior doctor even argued that if people were okay with paying exorbitant sums of money to dine at marquee restaurants, why was there so much angst about the prices charged by private hospitals! But others admit that even initiatives that were originally designed to streamline billing and make it more pocket friendly – such as introduction of packages for various diseases – have in the hands of unscrupulous practitioners become tools of exploitation.

Hospitals have no reason to check whether the billed procedures or packages have been delivered. It is for the patient or their families to watch out for discrepancies, though their ability to do so is limited by the quality and quantum of information that doctors give them. They might contest some of the charges but eventually end up paying the full amount of the bill, while they wait for a resolution of the complaint made either to the hospital or to an appellate authority.

Following up on these complaints requires perseverance that not everybody may have. Sometimes the matter is resolved long after the patient has passed away. That was the case with Ramsheela Bai, whose husband, Bishan Lal, received a refund 12 years after her death. The resident of Durg passed away in 2010, and the National Consumer Redressal Forum resolved the case only in

October 2023. This case reveals a lot about the malpractices of private hospitals.

Ramsheela Bai had been admitted to Apollo B.S.R. Hospital in Durg, following a heart problem diagnosis in a local nursing home. At Apollo, the family paid an initial deposit of ₹20,000, with the total treatment estimated to cost ₹85,000. Bishan Lal agreed to pay the amount. However, the next day, the doctor allegedly demanded ₹2,00,000, leaving him bewildered. When questioned about this sudden increase, the doctor did not offer a cogent explanation but insisted on immediate payment, claiming that it was crucial for his wife's health. After Bishan Lal paid the additional amount, his wife was moved to the ICU, and the family could only observe her from a distance. Bishan Lal alleged that he was not kept informed about her actual condition. The doctor and hospital staff had assured him that her health was improving, until she suddenly died four days after her admission.

The hospital then informed Bishan Lal that the total bill was ₹2,94,260, and they would only release the dead body upon the payment of the remaining ₹74,260. After much pleading, Bishan Lal managed to claim his wife's body by depositing an additional ₹50,000. But when he requested a detailed breakdown of the expenses and information about the treatment provided, the hospital failed to provide any documents or explanations, he mentioned in his complaint to the forum. This lack of transparency coupled with the significant increase in the initially estimated fees led him to believe that the hospital had taken unfair advantage of his distress to extract extra money from him. That is why he went to the consumer commission.

The forum eventually ruled that the hospital's actions constituted a deficiency in service and professional misconduct. It had exploited the complainant's vulnerability and lack of knowledge to overcharge for various services and treatments through misleading and deceptive means, thereby violating service terms.[7] The initial admission, the forum noted, had been for a ₹85,000 package but the final bill added another ₹2,09,260 to it. Bishan Lal was awarded a refund of ₹2,70,000 by district consumer forum but the national forum revised that to ₹1,85,000. This was the amount charged in excess of the original ₹85,000 that the patient's family had agreed to. It was found during the hearings that no information regarding what was included or excluded in the package was given to Bishan Lal. It was only when the apex forum asked for the details did the hospital provide a brochure. This opacity is standard practice in many private hospitals.

In Lal's case, the package included charges for hospital stay (one day in the ICU and two days in the Ward), inpatient nursing and dietician charges, cath lab charge, cardiologist's fee, and consultation fee for the stay and for specified routine investigations. It did not include charges for inpatient stay of more than three days, take-home medications, fees of other doctors, additional cath lab consumables or tests, medicines and consumables above a defined limit, high value medicines, cost of stent and the angioplasty balloon in case it needed to be used. It also did not include the cost of investigations that are not a part of the package. The exclusions were significant, and the bigger problem was that all this information was given 13 years later.

The forum noted that detailed information about the contents of the ₹85,000 package should have been provided to the patient. It also emphasised that using the term 'package' implies that it covers the entire treatment, regardless of the duration of hospitalisation and therefore the hospital did not have the right to demand any additional amount from Bishan Lal. The hospital could not submit any documentary evidence that they had informed the patient that additional expenses would be billed separately. This was the ground used to rule that any attempt to recover additional amounts for the patient's treatment constituted an inappropriate use of a 'package' option.

This level of scrutiny of a hospital bill is beyond the capacity of most patients. Only transparent third-party audit of prescriptions and bills can detect such practices. But there is no provision for that because neither governments nor hospitals feel obliged to insulate patients' interests from corporate profiteering.

As medicine is advancing, hospital charges too are evolving. There is, for example, a class of medicines known as biologics – these are products that are derived from living organisms and administered as drugs or vaccines. A senior doctor explains: 'If a patient is admitted for, say, rheumatoid arthritis or any chronic disease or cancer then he may be put on biologics, and doctors can charge him for administration of a drug like Infliximab (for RA) or hormonal therapy for cancer.' This charge is usually not disclosed in advance.

A surgeon can, at their own discretion, bill a patient for dressing a wound, and this charge is linked to room rent too. It is scarcely possible for patients or their families to keep count of the number of times a doctor dresses the wound. This is also a recurring charge that is difficult to verify for patients who develop bedsores. Each dressing charge can be as high as ₹10,000 to ₹15,000 for a patient admitted in a single occupancy room.

Milking the peripherals

The comparison of hospitals with hotels is not entirely misplaced. Like a hotel, a hospital needs to have services of laundry, housekeeping and catering. Until recently, most of these services were outsourced to small service provider companies. That is no longer the case. With scant government scrutiny, mega healthcare corporations now farm out non-clinical services to affiliates or to companies with linked ownerships. There is no legal hurdle to outsourcing, say, the washing of hospital linen or the collection and processing of hospital waste to a different company, nor is there any bar on procuring non-medical or medical consumables from an external entity. It only becomes a matter of regulatory oversight when such outsourcing impacts the cost of healthcare for patients.

For example, if a hospital outsources its catering to a company that charges significantly more than other similar companies and that cost is passed on to the patients, then there is a case for additional scrutiny or intervention. That is because these items contribute to overall healthcare inflation and have implications for companies listed on the bourse. But even in hospitals where governments have a stake or there are government representatives sitting on their boards, these matters of corporate governance are often ignored. The reasons for that may not be hard to fathom but that would take us to the realm of speculation.

A senior manager at a big healthcare chain reveals that when a few years ago they changed the caterers in their hospitals, there was a clear cost escalation. 'The patients get the same quality of food that they were getting earlier, but the hospitals are paying several times more for the catering. The new company also has linked ownerships with us and RFP conditions are framed clearly with this one company in mind so that nobody else qualifies to submit a bid,' he says. 'In any other industry, this would have been a corporate red flag but here nobody seems to notice anything amiss.' Hospitals have also begun reducing the number of housekeeping staff on their rolls to boost bottom lines. Instead, they are outsourced, sometimes to external companies that are subsidiaries of the parent entity.

Earlier, the costs of food and attendants were automatically included as part of the daily bed-and-nursing charges at hospitals. But of late, many hospitals – particularly the smaller ones, which are feeling the pinch more – are asking patients to engage 'verified' housekeeping staff from an 'internal pool'. The patients need to pay for these attendants separately, and the cost is usually not covered under medical insurance. This is one of the ways hospitals are passing on the costs to patients that the establishment used to bear earlier.

In some hospitals, non-medical consumables such as soaps, toothpaste and toilet paper are bought at higher-than-market rates from a sister company. Unlike in the government sector, there is no legal requirement for private limited companies to procure such items from the company quoting the lowest price though internal compliance and audit mechanisms may raise questions. These items are then billed to the patient under a generic category, without a breakup of how much individual items may cost. Any link between the promoters of the two business entities may not be common knowledge but it is not classified information either. A cursory glance through annual reports available in the public domain is enough to establish the links. Any government that wants to act on this potentially problematic practice does not lack the information or evidence but perhaps simply the will to act.

This reluctance was highlighted on 19 March 2024, when the central government was forced to convene a meeting with state governments to discuss healthcare costs after coming under fire from the Supreme Court about the unregulated and opaque pricing structures of private hospitals. The case had been filed by an organisation called the Veterans Forum for Transparency in Public Life. It has made the government of India start a rather belated process of exploring whether prices could be fixed. In the meeting held at Nirman Bhawan, several states opposed the idea. The minutes of the meeting were filed as part of the Centre's response to the Supreme Court.

The minutes show that Haryana, Bihar, Telangana and Mizoram were among the states that requested wider consultations with all stakeholders, including private players, before any decisions on price fixation were taken. Officials from Bihar and Mizoram also suggested that organisations such as the Indian Medical Association could be involved in this process, while officials from Gujarat and Madhya Pradesh said that fixing of rates may lead to serious compromises in the quality of healthcare and treatment of patients, particularly in the private sector. Officials from Uttar Pradesh believed that fixed rates may lead to serious issues which would render some healthcare setups financially unviable, while officials from Uttarakhand were concerned that any such action would make the healthcare sector uncompetitive, 'considering the economic dynamics and interaction of market forces'.

Ambulances

Last mile connectivity is a very important metric for urban planning. Unfortunately, ambulances, which provide last mile connectivity for health systems, are poorly regulated both in terms of the quality of services they offer and the prices they charge. The ramshackle Maruti Omnis that ply in the name of ambulances in most city streets are a far cry from an ideal means of transport for patients. Despite it being common knowledge that a well-equipped ambulance could save lives, it has been a neglected aspect of public health. Step out of the urban jungle and the conditions of these emergency vehicles get worse, with barely any equipment or manpower supporting them. Almost all states now have a helpline number to call for a properly maintained and staffed ambulance, operated by the National Health Mission (NHM) – the biggest health programme run jointly by the central and state governments. However, NHM ambulances have limited availability. The number of vehicles is inadequate; they often do not ply beyond regular office hours. The quality of equipment and manpower too leave much to be desired. A 2020 analysis of publicly funded ambulances, published in *Clinical Epidemiology and Global Health,* found that 32 per cent of the vehicles did not meet standards while a shocking 71 per cent of the emergency medical technicians who man them had below average knowledge.[8] Among the substandard ambulances, 66.7 per cent had technicians with below average knowledge. A 2022 report by NITI Aayog and the Jai Prakash Narayan Trauma Centre in AIIMS Delhi gave an even more dismal picture, where it found that while 91 per cent of tertiary and secondary care hospitals have in-house ambulances, only 34 per cent of them have trained paramedics.[9] Comparing India to 'US of the 1960s', it estimated that 98.5 per cent ambulance runs in the country were for transporting dead bodies, thanks to the high number of road traffic accidents. An estimated 90 per cent ambulances are without any equipment or oxygen.

Big corporate hospital chains have their own ambulances, with trained manpower and high-end equipment, but they are neither enough in number to cater to the entire population, nor are they affordable.

This allows largely unregulated private ambulance services to step in and quote any price they wish in an emergency. This is particularly true in remote or rural areas where health services may be less accessible. Most of them are little more than a mode of conveyance, because their life-saving capabilities are limited or non-existent.

On Indian roads, even in the big cities, motorists often give way to an ambulance only to find that the vehicle is in such poor state that it cannot even accelerate enough to pass them. In these vehicles, instead of trained paramedical personnel, it is the family member of the sick person who must provide whatever support they can to the patient during the journey to the hospital.

Ambulances are called for when people are at their most vulnerable; the charges quoted can be proportionate to the seriousness of the medical emergency and the availability of alternate means of reaching a health facility. This is why ambulances started charging unheard of rates during the COVID-19 pandemic; it went as high as ₹40,000 per trip in the National Capital Region (NCR). Many governments and district administrations tried to regulate charges by notifying formal rates which could not be exceeded. The average rate was ₹25 per kilometre for an air-conditioned ambulance and ₹20 per kilometre for one without AC. The Delhi government, for example, mandated that ambulances could charge ₹1,500 to ₹4,000 for a distance of up to ten kilometres, after which a surcharge would be applicable. Some of these orders continue to be in force but are violated with impunity.

While some private health insurers cover ambulance expenses, the PMJAY does not include the cost of patient transport. This is ironic as most of the scheme's target beneficiaries are the urban poor and residents of smaller towns and villages for whom the cost of reaching a health facility on top of the loss of a day's wages – a hospital trip in a village can take an entire day – can be a serious deterrent to care-seeking behaviour. Corporate hospitals, meanwhile, have moved on to a whole new level of patient transport, with the advent of air ambulances. These choppers are regulated as a commercial air service.[10] The civil aviation ministry has strict regulations regarding the maintenance of the aircraft, the medical equipment, the crew members and the trained healthcare personnel on board. But the regulations do not set any limit for the charges of air ambulances, leaving it once again on the market to decide. Hourly rates for an air ambulance can vary from ₹60,000 to ₹65,000 per hour to ₹2 lakh. Even though there is periodic outrage in the country whenever there is a spike in fares for regular commercial flights, exorbitant charges for air ambulances never make it to mainstream conversations. They may be the chosen vehicles for the well-heeled, but air ambulances save lives too and some of the arguments in favour of price regulation in the healthcare space equally apply to them.

From Omnis to choppers, the diverse range of ambulances in the country reflects the wide chasm between private hospitals and government healthcare facilities when it comes to service quality and costs. As India looks for ways to make healthcare accessible and affordable for its 1.4 billion population, patient transport facilities can be a microcosm where models of affordability, accessibility and quality care can be piloted and eventually scaled up once their efficiency is proven.

5

To Refer or Not to Refer

There is something reassuring about the white coat, calm demeanour and the ready smile of a doctor, as they listen to all that is ailing you and tell you that they can make it all go away. This promise of succour is what families bank on when a doctor asks a patient if they would like to have a colleague take a second look at the patient. Thanks to Google, conversations around questionable medical ethics and awareness that clinical competence may vary from one doctor to another, the value of getting a second opinion has now been firmly established.

Only, like a lot of other things in healthcare, referral decisions may or may not be disinterested. There can be occasions when the doctor might genuinely feel out of depth or feel the need to brainstorm with a colleague to decide the best course for a patient; but there are also times when the decision is taken because there are more than just clinical considerations. Sometimes doctors will refer patients to each other – known as cross-referrals – a practice that is in the crosshairs of both the National Medical Commission and health insurance providers.

This thin line between necessary and unnecessary referrals has become even less discernible with the emergence of super specialisations splitting medical disciplines as we once knew them into narrower streams; for example, an orthopaedic surgeon may legitimately take the position that as a knee specialist they would not be able to guide the patient on what recourse to take for a complaint of frozen shoulder and thus refer the patient to a doctor who only works on shoulder joints. Moving on from specialist doctors, there are now a flurry of single specialty hospitals in fields such as oncology, dentistry, paediatrics and fertility treatments. Industry watchers feel that this is the direction the Indian health sector might increasingly take in the future. Earlier, the old-fashioned general physician, referred to as the family physician, was almost an omniscient generalist willing to deal with nearly every ailment, including those of the mind. His unique relationship and knowledge of the family in fact made him best suited for this. However, the new age specialist is loath to explore beyond the confines of their domain, opening the floodgates of referrals across departments.

A doctor who has spent close to two decades at a top Delhi hospital claims that the decision to refer is subjective, because there are no clear guidelines – either from the government or at the level of individual establishments – on when to give a referral. 'If a patient comes to the hospital for an orthopaedic procedure and is found to have low sodium levels,' he says, 'should the primary doctor, which in this case would probably be an orthopaedic surgeon, refer the patient to a doctor in the internal medicine department? If he does, there is nothing unethical about it. It is not against any rules. Yet, it is also true that fluid management, which could fix the sodium levels, is one of the most basic lessons that we are taught at medical school. It does not require some exotic intervention from another discipline. Similarly, if a patient is admitted in cardiology and complains of vertigo, an ENT referral will inevitably follow, but the truth is that it may be quite manageable for the primary doctor to look at.'

At times referrals are given from a clinical discipline to its surgical counterpart, like when a gastroenterologist refers a patient to a gastrointestinal surgeon. But a layman has no way to assess if it is necessary or if the referral is an outcome of a quid pro quo between the clinician and the surgeon. 'Only hospital insiders know that the two doctors refer patients to each other; no patient would be able to understand this,' the doctor points out. 'The patient feels well cared for, being seen by four or five doctors every day, but for prolonged hospitalisation the charges by all of them can cumulatively send the final invoice spiralling up. Whether or not referrals are warranted, they have become standard practice in corporate hospitals. Doctors can charge a fee merely by signing the case file after recording a reason for the referral, sometimes without even talking to the patient.

Occasionally, unscrupulous consultants will even have a junior doctor forge their signature. One signature equals one visitation charge. But it is important to understand that not all referrals are unnecessary; some can be lifesavers. Others are done as part of the practice of defensive medicine which doctors assess is equally due to falling clinical standards and a fear of litigation. 'Sometimes doctors are not confident about their own diagnosis,' reveals a Delhi-based intensivist, who is one of the prominent voices on medical ethics. 'So they follow the guidelines to the letter, ensuring that they would be able to defend a particular clinical decision in court, if it came to that. This can cause unnecessary referrals within the same hospital.'

However, the intensivist points out that many of these guidelines have been developed in countries whose healthcare systems are very different from ours. There is a lot more public spending on healthcare in those countries, where the government enforces diagnosis and treatment protocols that may add to healthcare costs, but it also bears most of that expenditure. Citizens spend little to nothing out of pocket, though they may sometimes have to wait a while before they can access the care they need. 'To implement those same norms in India may have severe cost implications and can be debilitating for patients without insurance,' he says.

Moreover, in India's corporate hospitals, there is no standard process of cancelling a referral once it has been given. Therefore, the referred doctor could continue to visit and bill the patient for as long as they are admitted. There are some doctors who will not do further consultations once the complaint has been dealt with, thereby not charging any additional fees. Others may be less conscientious. Imagine a situation where a patient getting admitted for a planned surgery gets diagnosed with a mild fever or low haemoglobin during the routine pre-surgery tests. An internal medicine referral is in order. But once the fever is managed or the haemoglobin brought to a level where surgery is safe and has been performed, the surgeon is fully competent to take over. But rarely will a physician stop visiting on their own. It is only an alert patient or family member who could notice something amiss and question the doctor about these additional visits. One way of assessing whether a doctor's visits are necessary may be to monitor the medicines that are being administered to the patient.

A resident doctor at a corporate hospital recalls the time when a patient's son, who was carefully tracking his father's medications, bluntly asked a consultant physician why his visits continued even though the patient was no longer taking the medicines that he had prescribed. The consultant did not have a cogent reply, but he stopped visiting the patient after that. The business of referrals is so murky that some hospitals have now mandated that no patient can receive more than two visits a day by doctors from the same department. But compliance and oversight are both lax. Finding loopholes in rules is a specialty in its own right in the Indian healthcare system!

In July 2024, the West Bengal Clinical Establishment Regulatory Commission ruled on a case where a patient had been admitted to AMRI Hospital in Mukundapur in a vegetative state. The patient had stayed in the hospital for 22 days and was billed a total of ₹9,18,346, of which ₹19,500 was the consultancy fee of the anaesthesia specialist. The commission noted that the hospital had not been able to submit any plausible explanation as to why the anaesthetist, who assisted the neurosurgeon for a procedure that the patient had to undergo, had been charged for separately for 13 days, at the rate of ₹1,500 per day. The commission examined the notes of the patient (the papers that hang at the side of a hospital bed) and did not find any note by the doctor in question. It did not allow the hospital to charge for those visits.[1] The case established that a doctor who claims to have visited a patient but has not recorded their observations or advice in the patient's file cannot charge a fee for that visit.

What was also striking in this case was that the patient had been billed for 52 litres of mineral water, leading the commission to wonder how a patient in a vegetative state could possibly consume such huge amounts of water. It dismissed the hospital's contention that the mineral water may have been used for diluting the medicine. Incidentally, medicines are diluted using sterile water and not mineral water.

Elephant in the room

Why do doctors give unnecessary referrals? The answer to that question is neither easy nor comfortable. According to Dr Amar Jesani, former editor of the *Indian Journal of Medical Ethics* and a leading scholar on the topic, it can be traced back to a structural asymmetry in the early days of India's independence. 'The healthcare sector was still nascent in the 1960s, and the focus was on how to produce more doctors than on how to strengthen the healthcare system,' he explains. 'Yet, the system was not really in a position to absorb all the doctors that were being produced every year. About 25 per cent of medical graduates got government jobs, but others had to build their own practices. Basically, they had no option but to become entrepreneurs.'

This was before the advent of health insurance in India; moreover, big cities were the only places where people could afford to pay for healthcare. Cities therefore became the default destination for all doctors looking to make a living. 'To compete, they evolved a fee-for-service system in which they would pay other medical practitioners including alternative medicine practitioners to refer patients to them,' says Dr Jesani. 'Unlike other kinds of markets, the healthcare market is not driven by the consumer but by the seller. A patient, who is the consumer, will do what their doctor – the seller – advises them to do. That is why privatisation of healthcare is problematic. Prices do not necessarily come down when there are more providers. The competition may actually inflate the cost of healthcare.'

This is often seen in the intra-hospital referral dynamics in the private sector, where each doctor is looking out for their 'friends' with the hope or understanding that the favour will be returned. Dr Jesani uses the example of a fresh MBBS graduate trying to set up their practice to explain how this cascade of commissions works. 'Where does the young doctor get patients from? Nobody knows them, and there is no reason for patients to walk into a newly opened clinic,' he proffers. This is another way healthcare is different from other businesses; people may want to visit a new restaurant or shop to experience something new, but for health advice they will always prefer to consult only a tried and trusted doctor, making it extremely difficult for a new entrant to establish themselves.

Dr Jesani explains: 'The only way for this new doctor to build their practice is to visit all the other allopathy, homoeopathy, Ayurvedic and Unani doctors in that area, introduce themselves and request referrals. Should these other doctors refer patients to the new clinic, they would get a "cut" from the consultation fees that they get from the referred patient.' This is despite fee splitting – the practice of doctors referring patients to others and getting a part of the fees – being illegal in India. It remains an open secret among private practitioners in both small towns and big cities, primarily because it is very difficult to detect. In small towns, fee splitting may take on a slightly different form, with pathology laboratories, small nursing homes and independent practitioners getting into the mix.

Dr Jesani says some of the first independent hospitals to be set up in India were maternity hospitals, which went about establishing their business using a slightly expanded version of this model. They would reach out to individual obstetrics and gynaecology specialists asking them to send patients to their establishment. The specialists on their part needed a fully functioning OT to perform a caesarean section if needed. So, the deal was that if they referred patients to the hospital, they would also be allowed to perform the surgery there. That way they could profit from both the surgery fees and the commission from the overall bill. 'The individual practitioners were paying cuts down the chain and taking cuts from above,' says Dr Jesani. 'As the healthcare system expanded and larger conglomerates came about, healthcare continued to get more expensive because commissions downstream started being built into the pricing model.'

As the entities got bigger in size, they also started gobbling up the competition. Smaller establishments disappeared, allowing large corporates to establish virtual monopolies. This allowed them to dictate prices. The practice of commissions has now evolved into an all-pervasive presence in the healthcare system in the country, with few willing to openly acknowledge the proverbial elephant in the room. It took someone from outside the system to highlight the problem. Dr David Berger, an Australian primary care physician, spent some time working in India. He later wrote a series of scathing indictments in the *BMJ* about the bribes, illegal commissions and unethical practices that he found in the Indian healthcare system.[2]

In his pieces, Dr Berger wrote about the time when in the outpatient department of a government hospital, he was writing a recommendation for an exercise electrocardiogram (ECG) at a private heart clinic. A young resident who was working with him said, 'Give me that, I have to sign it.' Perplexed, Dr Berger handed it over. It took a little probing for him to understand the urgency. All investigations, he found, attract 10 per cent to 15 per cent kickback to the referring doctor. The marketing executive of the clinic would periodically turn up at the hospital with envelopes full of cash – the commissions for the doctors who had ordered tests from there. Berger wrote:

> The senior doctor refused it and stipulated that in the future the commission was to be paid back to patients, which is why the resident had to sign the form. The country's doctors and medical institutions live in an "unvirtuous circle" of referral and kickback that poisons their integrity and destroys any chance of a trusting relationship with their patients.

Dr Berger had witnessed a very common affliction of the Indian health system. Young resident doctors on their first jobs at hospitals would find sealed envelopes delivered to them after they had referred patients to a particular laboratory without expecting any inducements. The envelope had cash – paid as per the going 'rate' for referral – and sometimes a note with the proposition to keep the 'partnership' going. Some succumbed to that lure of easy money; many did not. A doctor who worked as a resident at a hospital in Delhi's diplomatic enclave over two decades ago was offered ₹1,000 to ₹1,500 by a pathological laboratory for every referral he wrote, depending on how pricey the tests were. He admits that it was good money for a young person on a monthly salary of ₹18,000. 'I told the guy to pass the benefit on to the patient. But many of my colleagues made five thousand to six thousand extra a month,' he reveals.

Lawyer Ashok Aggarwal claims that in many government hospitals the staff are in no hurry to repair diagnostic machines once they develop a snag. 'This applies even to the most expensive and latest equipment,' he says. 'If they keep the machines in working condition then they have to actually work and only get paid their salary, but by referring patients to private laboratories, they get extra income without doing any work. They also still get their fixed salary because they can simply claim that the machines are out of order.'

Industry insiders estimate that about 30 per cent to 60 per cent of the price of diagnostic tests – depending on their value and the frequency at which they are prescribed – is paid as commission to the doctor who prescribes the test and refers the patient to the diagnostic centre. The rate of commission can also vary depending on the location, the clout of the diagnostic laboratory and the stature of the doctor. In smaller cities, the doctor has a bigger influence on patients and hence can quote their own price. Diagnostic laboratories have to comply or risk losing out to a rival centre. Even cities such as Delhi, where the patient is much more aware of their options, a commission for the prescribing doctor is usually factored into the prices of tests. Thus, it is possible, even easy, to wrangle a discount from a laboratory by saying that you do not have a physical prescription from the doctor and were advised the test on a telephonic consultation!

'Some doctors literally carry a little black book in which they maintain a list of all their prescribed tests and then consult it diligently when it is time to receive commissions,' reveals a doctor who has been working in this sector for over two decades. 'Some are so particular about the laboratory at which the tests should be done that they will rip up the reports if the patient dares to go to a different lab!' But he concedes that there are also doctors who will let a patient do the tests from wherever they want. This is more common in the bigger cities.

Even in this artificially inflated market, some healthcare businesses have managed to buck the trend and lower their charges by charting their own course. House of Diagnostics (HOD), a chain of diagnostic labs that has been around since 2008–2009 is one such market disruptor. Dr Shubham Sogani, the CEO of HOD, shares that they were months away from selling off the business in 2014 as it was not doing well, and that was when the company decided to drastically change their ways of conducting business.

They stopped reaching out to doctors to get referrals and instead started targeting patients directly, trying to attract them by advertising discounts. By changing their business model, they saved on paying commissions to doctors. 'We shifted our focus and passed the resultant savings to the patients in the form of discounts,' says Dr Sogani. 'The market, which is inherently inflated, doesn't have any logic behind diagnostic costs that are being charged to patients, so there was no benchmark to set our rates. We had to laboriously work out our costs so that we were a viable business without burdening patients unnecessarily. We set our costs keeping in mind our running expenses, salaries and a markup to ensure sustainability. Our rates are fixed and way below the market prices. At the time when CGHS, which often draws flak from private hospitals for the low rates that it offers, was paying PET-CT charges at around ₹24,000, we were offering the scan at half that price. Our rates are on average 40 per cent to 60 per cent lower than what is charged by others. We have grown from strength to strength.'

In corporate hospitals, some of these commission-based models of bringing in business, are often institutionalised. That was why Mumbai's Asian Heart Institute caused a huge furore in 2017 when it put up a billboard advertisement with the tagline: 'Honest Opinion, No Commission to Doctors'. It was perhaps the first time a corporate hospital in India had openly admitted to the practice of giving commissions to doctors based on the amount of revenue they generated from admitting patients, prescribing diagnostic tests or performing surgeries. Despite tremendous backlash from his own professional community, the owner of the hospital, Dr Ramakant Panda, stood his ground.[3] He did not change his stance even when his detractors accused him of showing his peers in poor light and making a virtue out of a physician's commitment to ethical practice, as embodied in the Hippocratic Oath.

Discernible patterns in intra-hospital referrals point towards systemic problems that are ignored despite being common knowledge within the institution. 'There is an element of unstated quid pro quo in intra-hospital referrals, and many of them may not be necessary. There are patterns – if one cardiologist refers patients to a particular respiratory medicine specialist, chances are the latter is also returning the favour. There will be several disparate groups of doctors who will refer patients only within their own group,' explains a senior surgeon. 'There is nothing wrong in that because professionals prefer to work where there is a certain comfort level and trust in each other's judgement. Interdisciplinary approach is a cornerstone of modern medicine. But it is when there is repeated and predictable reciprocity that there is a red flag. There is nothing in the hospital setup that can detect or keep track of these patterns.'

When physicians give referrals to each other, the mathematics is straightforward because each doctor demands consultancy fees as per the hospital rates. But when it comes to surgeons, this is a little more complicated. Surgeons get paid a considerably larger sum of money for every surgery they perform compared to the daily fees that physicians get paid for visiting an inpatient. While rates vary, on average, about 25 per cent of the total charges for surgery is the surgeon's fee. Usually, patients consult a physician first and are then referred to a surgeon, so even though in most cases the physician is the primary doctor, it is the surgeon who makes more money if surgery is required.

For example, for a surgery with a fee of ₹4 lakh, the surgeon earns about ₹1 lakh. In comparison, a physician who charges ₹1,500 per visit makes a measly ₹12,000 after visiting an inpatient twice a day during a four-day hospital stay. This disparity is sometimes exploited by surgeons who offer a part of their own fees to clinical specialists in related fields in return for sending patients their way. Surgeons and physicians who form such a link can ensure that there is a steady flow of income for both. A physician would then refer a patient only to the surgeon with whom they have an 'arrangement'.

Some years ago, a prominent corporate hospital chain realised that many of their surgeons had made such arrangements for exclusive patient referrals with some of their physicians. This led to those surgeons doing back-to-back surgeries every day, while others who did not indulge in this practice were left without any surgical assignments. For the hospital, salaried surgeons sitting idle were a wasted resource. A senior administrator who was privy to the internal discussions on optimum use of human resources reveals that after many deliberations the administration concluded that there was a need to institutionalise fixed bonuses for physicians for admitting a patient and then referring them for surgery.

After several rounds of negotiations, a 25 per cent fee was agreed as a 'standby charge' to be paid to the consulting physician who referred the patient to the surgeon. Half of this fee would be paid by the surgeon, who would now make 12.5 per cent of the total surgery fee instead of the earlier 25 per cent. The remaining 12.5 per cent to be paid to the physician would be levied on the patient. 'We thus ensured that there was transparency without making the patient pay for it,' claims the administrator. Strictly speaking this claim is not entirely correct because from the patient's point of view, the surgery cost just went up by 12.5 per cent!

The tussle for surgery patients can lead to bad blood between surgeons if a patient switches surgeons at the last minute. A doctor at a corporate hospital in Delhi recounted an instance in his hospital where the patient after having a few consultations with one surgeon, chose to go to another one in the same hospital. After the surgery, when the patient had been shifted to the room the surgeon they had originally consulted barged in one day to berate them about the switch. The patient was still groggy post-anesthesia and was naturally taken aback by this aggression. The family lodged a complaint with the hospital management. "The administration was split on the issue,' reveals the doctor. 'Some senior officials felt that the surgeon was justifiably upset at their patient having chosen a colleague over them. But others pointed out that by law it was the right of the patient to choose their surgeon, and such instances of misbehaviour with the patient could only serve to bring a bad name to the hospital.'

But the power to refer patients is not the sole remit of doctors. Sometimes, people from rural or remote areas travel to bigger cities seeking treatment for an ailment without being sure of which doctor to go to. This is true of cities like Delhi, Kolkata, Mumbai, which see a significant annual influx of sick people in search of a good doctor. Who they end up with can be decided by a myriad bunch of individuals, included among them the auto rickshaw driver or rickshaw puller who will take them to the hospital and the receptionist there who will decide which doctor to send them to. A doctor who has studied and practised in Kolkata reveals that at several big hospitals in that city, the hospital receptionist holds a very influential position. 'The consultant doctors make sure that they have excellent working relationships with the people that staff the reception desk because they are the ones who will send patients to them,' he says. 'It is not uncommon to buy the receptionist's favour using cash or some other form of inducement. In return, when a patient turns up without a specific doctor in mind, the receptionist will recommend that they see the doctor who has been the most generous to them.' Even if the patient wants to see a particular doctor, the receptionist might deftly send them in another direction if they are so inclined. They might tell the patient that the doctor of their choice was not in so they can either come back later or they can choose to see somebody else who is 'just as good or even better and is available right now'. Few patients choose to come back later.

In smaller towns, healthcare is less organised, insurance penetration is lower and awareness levels are poorer when compared to metro cities. Those connected to the transport sector are the preferred collaborators for small and mid-sized hospitals. Hospitals will often offer a small commission to the town's ambulance staff to ensure that any emergency patients are brought to them.

Referral guidelines

Though the erstwhile Medical Commission of India (now National Commission of India) issued an explicit directive against referrals, at a policy level the approach in India is that doctors need to do more referrals, not less. That is because health policy in India is drafted largely with government hospitals in mind. Private hospitals inexplicably are kept out of such directives, with some exceptions being made when there is public hue and cry. There is a vast difference between how medicine is practised in government and private hospitals. In government hospitals, doctors are more rushed because they have to see the same number of patients in a day that doctors in a private hospital probably see in a week. Anybody who has tried to take a patient to an OPD in any government hospital, particularly in a big city, would have negotiated the endless queues and occasional jostling. Doctors in government hospitals rarely give referrals, not because they don't want to to gain financially but because it may cause additional delay in starting the treatment. This is crucial as patients often reach them when the disease has grown and getting the treatment started takes precedence over everything else. Inpatient care is mostly handled by resident doctors, whose hours of continuous duty can range from 24 to 48 hours. They may be too inexperienced or stressed or in awe of seniors to push for referrals.

In 2016, Maya Acharya was admitted to one of the best government medical institutes in the country for a knee replacement surgery. Maya had been a hypertensive for almost 25 years, but her blood pressure had been very well controlled by her primary care physician in her hometown. At the medical institute, she was assured that her orthopaedic surgeon was among the best in the country, and despite her long medical history of high blood pressure, no internal medicine referral was given. The surgery went well, physiotherapy started as usual. But when she was being discharged, it was not the senior surgeon who had done the surgery but a younger orthopaedics resident doctor who wrote Maya's discharge summary, detailing her medications and rehabilitation protocol. In it, he had changed all her blood pressure medications.

Three days later, Maya had to be rushed to a corporate hospital near her home after her blood pressure shot to 220/110 from her usual 140/90. A combination of blood pressure lowering medicines and diuretics (that increase the frequency of urination and lower the fluid load of the body) brought her BP down within a short time, but when doctors got down to analysing what had caused the spike, they zeroed in on the changed medications. The orthopaedics resident had replaced Maya's blood pressure medicines with medicines of far lower potency and different active ingredients. One of those doctors explained that if a patient has had high blood pressure for a long time, the medicines may have to be changed or the dosage adjusted periodically because the body may not always respond in the same manner to the same medicine if they are taken continuously for years.

So, a patient like Maya, who was on blood pressure medication for 25 years, the ideal combinations of drugs and dosages would have taken some deliberation and some trial and error by her primary care physician. The orthopaedics resident had simply put her on introductory blood pressure drugs that her body had long grown out of. This was due to his lack of experience in internal medicine. It would have been better for Maya if an internal medicine or cardiology referral had been given.

There are many other cases like Maya's. That is why the health ministry issued guidelines in June 2024 mandating timely interdepartmental referrals of patients. The guidelines state that good patient care needs to be comprehensive because a patient can have multiple comorbid medical conditions or even a single medical condition with multisystem manifestations. 'For comprehensive medical care, inputs from different departments are essential, which requires a robust referral policy,' the guidelines declare, adding that efficient referral mechanisms should be an essential part of the training for resident doctors as well. 'Interdepartmental referrals also serve as opportunities for interdisciplinary collaboration and sharing of knowledge among healthcare providers,' the guidelines mention.[4]

There is one kind of patient that all hospitals, whether government or private, are eager to refer; it is the patient who may have deteriorated over a long period of hospitalisation to a point where survival is unlikely or one who may have suffered massive trauma such as a road accident with minimal chances of making it. The law requires hospitals to treat and manage trauma patients to a reasonable state of stability before being referred or transferred, but hospitals manage to find loopholes to bypass that regulation. In fact, at a prominent government medical institute in Delhi at one one point of time, ambulances were kept ready to quickly shift very sick patients to another lower-profile government hospital nearby so that the patient would not die on their watch. Private hospitals too find some pretext or another to refuse admission to patients who appear to be on the edge of a precipice on arrival.

The directorate general of health services has notified a referral policy for the Delhi NCR region which mandates that no patient would be referred out from one tertiary hospital to another except for services that are unavailable (as per the displayed Citizen Charter) at the first hospital. When this is done, prior communication to the destination hospital and their confirmation is required.[5] The ethics of referrals have been discussed at length in various medical journals and in revelatory books authored by doctors.

In their book *Dissenting Diagnosis*, published in 2016, Dr Arun Gadre and Dr Abhay Shukla wrote about how doctors make money by referring even the sickest of patients. The 'rates' can vary from a few hundred rupees for a simple specialist referral to anything between ₹30,000 and ₹40,000 for a more complex procedure such as a cardiac angioplasty. However, these doctors who have consistently turned the spotlight inwards to expose the fault lines in their own profession, continue to be outnumbered by colleagues who turn a blind eye to it. While the question of medical ethics has been discussed to some extent with reference to individual doctors, the bigger issue of questionable corporate practices has not faced the same level of scrutiny.

Therefore, in public perception doctors have become the nucleus of all medical corruption, while the bigger, more systemic practitioners evade scrutiny. For the patient the doctor is the face of the health system, embodying all that is good or bad. The irony of this is that despite the constraints under which India's healthcare system performs, it still manages to reach a substantial proportion of the population largely because of the commitment of individual medical practitioners, some of whom choose to relocate to remote locations with minimal financial incentives in the spirit of service. They, alongside those trusted foot soldiers of India's rural health mission – ASHA (Accredited Social Health Activists) workers – have made possible the impressive strides that India has made in various healthcare parameters in the last couple of decades.

6

Monitoring Is a Money-Spinner

Dr Ashish Singh is a senior doctor at a corporate hospital where he has been working for over two decades. But when his wife needed surgery, he chose to go to a different institution. He trusted the surgeon there more than his own colleagues. This is not unusual – when it comes to their own families, many doctors choose to go to colleagues whose skills they have faith in rather than stick to their own place of work where they may be tempted to make treatment decisions themselves. Concern about the welfare of a family member can sometimes cloud professional judgement.

When Mrs Singh was admitted, she brought along with all the usual hospital admission paraphernalia – medicines, clothes, toiletries – a bipap machine. She needed it for a health condition called obstructive sleep apnea, in which breathing sometimes momentarily stops while sleeping as the respiratory muscles relax and cause the airway to close. The commonest symptom of this is snoring. A bipap machine creates positive pressure so that the airway is kept open.

The machine is used intermittently, but once recommended for an admitted patient, the charges for a full day's use are added for the duration of the hospital stay, regardless of the hours of actual usage. The charges for a bipap machine for a week alone could allow the hospital to recover most of the purchase cost of the machine, which is in the range of ₹40,000 to ₹80,000. Dr Singh is familiar with the billing practices of corporate hospitals, and being part of the medical fraternity meant that his request to use his own machine rather than the one provided by the hospital was sympathetically dealt with. But for other patients who might need support from such a machine, such requests may not always be accepted. It is also true that few people may have an expensive equipment available at home.

The charges for continuous monitoring or use of a functional support machine can be a potent stressor for patients with financial constraints. Most people in India are yet unfamiliar with the concept of medical devices being commodities that are separately chargeable, so they remain blissfully unaware of the cost implications until the bill arrives. Such machines are major money-spinners for hospitals, not just within the premises but also at the homes of patients, now that many corporates have spun off a home care arm to take advantage of an ageing population with not enough caregivers at home. These rely on devices installed for remote monitoring and support as part of a home care package.

It is not just the charges for machines that add to the bill. One of the commonest parameters that doctors feel the need to monitor in a patient is blood sugar. If there is a need to check the sugar level every few hours – the file will usually say Random Blood Sugar (RBS). The utility of getting blood sugar reading several times a day, incidentally, is a matter of debate within the medical fraternity. But the direction to measure it continues to be fairly common. How much could it cost? After all, a glucometer sells for only a few hundred rupees, and the strips it uses could cost less than ₹10 each. It has, in recent years emerged as a common fixture in many middle-class households, much like oxymeters did in the aftermath of the COVID-19 pandemic. In a hospital, however, the financials change dramatically. Every prick of the finger is separately charged anything from ₹50 to a few hundred rupees. The category of bed is an important determinant of this charge. The opaque billing rules of private hospitals ensure that patients are never conscious of such small, incidental charges, and few feel the need to ask.

'If blood sugar is measured six times a day and the charges are ₹100 per reading then for a fortnight's hospitalisation the charges for blood sugar testing alone would add up to more than the fee for an ultrasound or a CT scan,' points out a former staff member of the billing department of a private hospital. 'But it is important to understand that the comparison with the cost of testing at home is not valid because in a hospital you are also paying for the nurse who takes the sample and measures it, the air conditioning, the infection control and hygiene measures, among other services. Should your readings be abnormal, management of the situation is going to be immediate in a hospital, unlike at home. So, a direct comparison is really like comparing apples and oranges.'

The disparity between a hospitals' charges for this service and to render their actual expenses – for consumables and manpower – is a problem area. According to a senior administrator at a prominent charitable hospital in South Delhi, the cost to the hospital for performing a blood sugar test is not more than ₹15 to ₹20 because the nurse who takes the sample is salaried and is not deputed exclusively to that patient and the strips for the test are procured in bulk and hence cost much less than what they sell for in the open market. 'Being a trust hospital, we do not put a margin on such things to keep the costs manageable,' he explains.

After COVID-19, public awareness increased about the importance of the hospital apparatus known as a ventilator. It is a form of functional support used for a patient who cannot maintain the correct air pressure in their lungs. Optimum air pressure levels are necessary to supply adequate oxygen to the entire body. The charges for putting a patient on a ventilator are very high. But the issue at stake is how much profit should a hospital be allowed to make off a patient fighting for their life?

According to a Delhi-based intensivist who has worked in government, corporate and charitable hospitals during a long career, world-class ICU care with a ventilator in a Tier 1 city costs about ₹30,000 to ₹35,000 per day in actuals for the hospital, with the ventilator charge component being about ₹2,000. He explains that in a charitable hospital, any profits are ploughed back into the hospital and there is no pressure to pay out dividends to shareholders;

so the patient pays about 15 per cent to 20 per cent more than the actual cost to the hospital. This markup is to cover things such as administrative expenses, utility bills and other incidentals. But in a corporate hospital, for the same kind of treatment in a well-equipped ICU, the patient can be billed anything in between ₹1 lakh and ₹1.5 lakh per day – the upper limit coming to about five times the cost to the hospital. 'There are many things that the patient is paying for there,' says the intensivist. 'The exorbitant salaries of the star doctors whose names bring in patients as well as that of the CEO who probably knows little about medicine but holds an MBA degree from a reputed institution. They are also paying for the latest equipment that the hospital boasts about on billboards, even though clinically speaking they may add very little value to the treatment.'

Some of these state-of-the-art medical devices are occasionally bought for bragging rights. If a hospital installs the first machine of its kind in the country or becomes the first hospital in the Southeast Asia region to boast of having it, they can issue a statement in the media about it, put out a few advertisements and get some coveted coverage. They can also put up advertisements across the city announcing this newest addition and what cutting-edge standards it bestows on patient care. The intensivist adds that hospitals do have legitimate expenses beyond what meets the eye, for them to continue to remain viable and fully functioning business entities. Ventilators, for example, are high maintenance units. The doctor explains that budgeting for routine downtime and unforeseen breakdowns, an ICU with 12 ventilator beds would probably need to buy 18 to 24 machines to keep all the beds operational at any given time.

Sometimes, hospitals make investments that do not produce the expected returns. The oxygen plants that were commissioned in the wake of the 2021 COVID-19 wave, triggered by the delta variant of the SARS-CoV-2 virus, commonly referred to as the second wave of the pandemic, rapidly became liabilities rather than assets. Private hospitals had to fall in line with government regulations that required even relatively small establishments to set up oxygen plants; in Ghaziabad, for example, the cut-off size for hospitals to produce their own oxygen was as low as 50 beds. Other states had different regulations. But after the pandemic, demand for oxygen waned and many plants fell into disuse, becoming bad investments over time. By April 2022, these plants were already being categorised in the highest echelons of the government as 'white elephants'.[1]

Doctors point out that while corporate hospitals may bear the brunt of criticism for their billing practices, they are the last bastions of quality in the private sector. A consultant doctor who recently quit a multi-centre corporate hospital for a smaller institution shared an appalling experience he had at his new place of work. 'I was treating a patient with a respiratory infection and during tests I found that he was low on one electrolyte – potassium,' he said. 'I prescribed potassium chloride to address the issue.' The next morning, the doctor was asked to rush to the hospital because the patient had deteriorated suddenly, and he had developed both tachycardia (high heart rate) and bradycardia (low heart rate). His heart rate was fluctuating wildly, and he was on the verge of collapse.

'Imagine my consternation when I found out that instead of administering the chemical through the saline that the patient was already being given, the staff had injected it!' said the doctor. 'It caused the electrolyte balance of the body to go completely awry. The patient survived, but it was sheer luck.' He concluded that though the bigger hospitals pay a pittance to the paramedical and support staff and even the junior doctors, they maintain a certain standard in the quality of service. That is why people continue to choose big corporate hospitals.

Gap in guidelines

In 2010, the Clinical Establishments Act came into force with the understanding that without uniform and enforceable standard treatment guidelines (STGs), clinical establishments could not possibly be held accountable. Doctors and hospitals would always hide behind the defence of subjectivity in clinical decision-making and the stance that action had been taken with the patient's best interests. Without STGs there was no benchmark against which to assess these decisions.

At present STGs exist for most specialties. However, what remains missing is an accountability structure that requires all doctors and hospitals to follow a uniform and common set of guidelines. Many big hospitals have their own protocols that have been developed internally or taken from international accreditation organisations such as the Joint Commission International. In the absence of validated, unified and mandatory Indian guidelines, top corporate hospitals and physicians look beyond our borders for treatment and diagnostic directions. Some of the most referred guidelines are those developed by the National Institute for Health and Care Excellence (NICE) in the United Kingdom or others from the US, Australia or the Scandinavian countries.

These are not adapted to the Indian context or developed specifically keeping the realities of Indian healthcare and resource constraints in mind, so they can can and often do end up having an inflationary effect on healthcare.

National Health Services (NHS) in the United Kingdom is a publicly funded healthcare programme that has often been cited as an example of a model healthcare system. It is going through a churn at present though, facing scrutiny and fund crunch, calling that proposition into question. Scandinavian countries too have an efficient, publicly-financed healthcare system with a high penetration of health insurance, while Australia has a universal public health insurance programme. The United States often figures in conversations about what could happen to healthcare with too much privatisation and reliance on market forces for price discovery.

A medical director who has been a vocal proponent of ethical medicine says that our government does not spend enough on healthcare. Also, with the entry and expansion of private healthcare, doctors are constantly worried about having to defend their clinical decisions in a court of law. 'In the absence of guidelines tailored for the health system in our country, doctors look to NICE or Scandinavian or Australian guidelines,' he says. 'But is the Indian patient ready to pay for the kind of services that governments in those countries pay for? The answer is no. It is for doctors to decide which tests to do, keeping in mind both the health and financial conditions of the patient. I also feel that doctors in general do not consider whether a patient can afford the test or the supportive intervention that they are prescribing. Some probably also lack the social sense to make that assessment.' He further adds: 'I also see a general lack of confidence among doctors in their own clinical judgements. It is not just that they are watching their own backs while ordering tests. Sometimes, without the test reports, they genuinely do not know what is happening.'

So, if foreign guidelines prescribe a liver or kidney function test or a complete blood count every few days, is it really necessary for Indian doctors to follow them? It depends on the doctor, but most of them agree that rationalising investigations both in admitted patients and those in the outpatient departments can be a very important tool to calm inflationary pressure on medical bills. This can dramatically impact the financial hit that a critically ill patient, or one looking at a long hospital stay, takes. Urinary tract infections (UTIs) are very common in old people and may require longer hospitalisation if the organism causing the infection is resistant to commonly used antibiotics. Drug resistance has now become common, thanks to years of unregulated over-the-counter sales of prescription antibiotics and a general lack of global awareness about the pitfalls of indiscriminate use of antibiotics. Sometimes, prolonged hospitalisation and compromised immunity – another common geriatric problem – leads to further hospital-acquired infections, also caused by drug resistant organisms. But unchecked use of advanced antibiotics can trigger further drug resistance. This is why it is crucial for a urologist to progress systematically, starting with what are known as first-line antibiotics. Depending on how the patient responds, the doctor could progress to second- and third-line drugs. The only way to find out what kind of organism has caused the UTI is a urine culture test, which tries to grow the bacteria from the patient's urine sample in laboratory conditions to identify and characterise it. This takes at least three days. However, because UTIs have a propensity to become serious very fast, and in an elderly person can precipitate a crisis, doctors usually start with a broad-spectrum antibiotic while waiting for the culture report.

A senior specialist in internal medicine says that it is possible that when the report comes three days later, the doctor finds the infection will not respond to the antibiotic course which was started. So, after finishing the minimum prescribed dose of that antibiotic, the patient needs to start another one that may work better. Whether it works or not can be conclusively proven only by another urine culture test. 'How frequently does one do these tests in case there is a patient who does not respond to the usual medicines?' These are clinical calls doctors take all the time, keeping in mind the patient's recovery. One doctor may decide on a frequency of tests that doesn't match another doctor's approach. Each approach would have a different impact on the final bill but cannot be faulted on that count alone.'

Arterial blood gas (ABG) is an important test for a patient who has been admitted with respiratory or circulatory problems. A blood sample is collected from the artery and analysed for oxygen and carbon dioxide quantities and pH (acidity/alkalinity) levels. These are important indicators of normal physiological functions. The test is moderately expensive but can give important information about the condition of the patient. It could be prescribed multiple times for a critical patient in need of monitoring to assess how well their lungs are functioning.

A senior respiratory medicine specialist explains that according to Western guidelines, the ABG test should be done every 48 hours. In some cases, it needs to be done every day. It costs around ₹2,000 for a test in a corporate hospital. 'This is where clinical judgement and empathy matter,' says the specialist. 'Doctors are beginning to err too much on the side of clinical overreaction, and this has implications for the overall cost of healthcare.'

After the COVID-19 pandemic, investors and businesses rediscovered the potential of healthcare as an avenue for assured returns. A prominent doctor-turned-entrepreneur frequently says in conversations within his organisation that investors 'queue up' to invest in his company. However, instead of making healthcare affordable for the common people, these investments have had an inflationary effect across the world. Simultaneously, a lot of startups have also come into the healthcare space. They offer tailored solutions for continuous care, benefitting significantly from outsourcing by corporate hospitals, which is a fairly recent phenomenon. But, here too, instead of lowering healthcare expenses, it has meant a bigger burden on the patients.

Patients who need to be in bed for long hours, or are unable to get up altogether, are at high risk of developing bed sores. For such patients, air mattresses are the preferred option. These come with an attached pump that keeps pushing air in and out so that the pressure points of the body on the mattress keep changing. This ensures that constant pressure at any one site does not bruise the skin. A patient who needs this type of mattress would have to pay a bed charge as per the hospital rates and then will be billed the rent for the air mattress separately. This rent can be as high as ₹3,500 per day. Another such high-rent item is an intermittent pneumatic compression device, which are reusable padded bandages used in surgery patients to prevent a condition called deep vein thrombosis (DVT). Deep vein thrombosis is the formation of clots in immobile patients; it needs to be prevented because this clot can dislodge and travel to other parts of the body, causing an obstruction of the blood supply if it gets stuck in a fine vessel. This can even cause a stroke. The rent can vary depending on the hospital and the class of bed. For patients who have a slow healing wound, a vac machine is used which can expedite healing by creating negative pressure around the wound. This is also charged separately on a per day basis.

An administration official at a private hospital reveals that hospitals do not buy such items anymore because the usage is relatively limited. 'They take them on rent from companies and charge patients at a higher rate to create a margin of profit while saving on the maintenance,' they say. 'The management professionals who have oversight on the billing process also work towards increased uptake of such devices. Doctors will get calls from them or from ancillary departments about add-ons such as physiotherapy sessions or support devices even when the doctor's note does not mention any such thing.' He warns that if a doctor is not conscious of the billing implications and agrees to these suggestions, the patient could easily be charged an extra ₹10,000 to ₹15,000 per day.

Home care

Remote healthcare took off in India in the wake of the COVID-19 pandemic, when the government started promoting telemedicine to ensure people with existing health conditions did not miss out on essential medical care. Remote care, however, is only as good as remote patient monitoring. Only when a doctor receives accurate information about a patient's vital parameters can they prescribe an appropriate course of treatment. Therefore, the recording of those parameters, whether done manually or with the use of technology, must be accurate.

In April 2020, AIIMS set up India's first remote health-monitoring centre in partnership with Bharat Electronics Limited to monitor the status of COVID-19 patients in Uttarakhand. After the pandemic, there was no immediate necessity for remote care but both telemedicine and remote monitoring quickly emerged as lucrative business propositions for the private sector. The advent of artificial intelligence (AI) in the healthcare space added an additional dimension to that conversation. AI or machine learning involves teaching machines to use reason and logic by using information fed into the system along with other pre-programmed functions.

AI is adept at reading and analysing large data sets but lacks the sagacity and experience of a doctor. Medical diagnosis involves a nuanced reading of not just the patient's reports and symptoms but also correlations with a host of other things including their personal and sometimes also professional situations. Sometimes something as basic as the gait of a patient can be revelatory to the trained eyes of a doctor. Complex decision-making skills of AI are still a work in progress which is why its medical conclusions need to be at present validated by a doctor.

Once the healthcare industry understood that AI could be a game changer in diagnosis and treatment of patients, it began to be used widely. For example, analysis of imaging tests, including X-rays and MRIs, for diagnosis of diseases such as TB and breast cancer using AI is one area where there has been a lot of progress. Among the most widespread commercial uses of AI in healthcare is its deployment for remote patient monitoring.[2] The setup and the monitoring mechanism varies but the broad principle remains the same. Sensors are used to monitor vital signs such as heart rate, respiratory rate, blood pressure and blood oxygen levels. These are recorded and displayed on a screen that can be at the same location as the patient or it can be remote. An alarm system is triggered should any of the readings deviate from the normal range, allowing quicker interventions to happen in patients who are away from the hospital.

For a home setup, the sensors could be in a wearable device such as a watch and the display/monitor at the most basic level can be a smartphone or a tablet computer. Various other kinds of devices have entered the market and are competing for a share in this small and niche segment. Some hospitals have already installed a remote monitoring system for each bed, while others are still testing waters, starting off with small numbers before they fully evaluate the pros and cons to take a call on scaling it up. Hospital beds with remote monitoring are of course steeply priced, with a generous margin for the hospital factored into the daily bed charges. The additional costs may not be covered by medical insurance, subject to the fine print of the policies' plans.

Another market that companies dealing in new-age remote monitoring devices are trying to target is that of the senior citizens living alone, often with children settled abroad who are willing to pitch in financially but are not always available to take on a more hands-on role in the care of their parents. Some of these senior citizens have trusted domestic staff who live with them. These attendants can take care of their daily needs but may not understand how to monitor their health status effectively. For this segment, mortality can be significantly reduced with an AI-powered device that can alert a designated person or group of people should any alarming fluctuations occur in the person's vitals.

Corporate hospitals are also vying for a slice of this same market by offering home care services. They have spotted business opportunities among the vulnerable geriatric population and are also cognisant of the vast potential that judicious use of technology holds in this space to improve both services and bottom lines. A posse of new-age, tech-driven companies have emerged as valuable allies for these corporate behemoths, perking up the market significantly. An executive at a company that rents out remote monitoring devices says that they charge a few thousand rupees a month as rental if the device is used in the home care setup. Once the patient's requirements have been met, they can return the device. However, corporate hospitals extract dual benefits from these devices. 'The devices make treatment decisions simpler, and there is not as much manual monitoring required,' he explains. 'That means that in the long term, hospitals can look at reducing staff strength and saving on salaries. The bonus for hospitals is that the devices are also a source of a significant amount of revenue. They pay us about ₹2,000 per device per bed per month but charge the patient about ₹1,000 to ₹1,200 per day per bed. They get 10x-12x revenue per month. Even with a 50 per cent occupancy in a month, that is an easy ₹1,5000 to ₹18,000 per month for the hospital of which very little is their actual outgo. For our device, insurance will usually cover the cost for the patient. But that is not the case with all such similar devices in the market,' he says. As bulk users, hospitals always have an upper hand – like they do with the pharmaceutical and med-tech industry – but when a company is just starting out with a new category of device that leverage is even more. A company that quotes higher rates will inevitably lose out.

Remote monitoring is sometimes recommended by hospitals as an alternative to ICU care. Shortening the duration of the hospital stay can provide succour to patients with limited financial means. The savings are massive – home care costs a few thousand rupees per day while an ICU in a corporate hospital could cost upwards of ₹1 lakh per day. The patient therefore readily accepts the recommendation for an AI-powered monitoring device from the hospital, unaware that it would be significantly cheaper were they to source it directly from the device manufacturer.

Remote monitoring is still a very nascent sector in India. The novelty value is yet to wear off and hospitals are still testing the waters on AI-based technology rather than going the whole distance in their adoption. The cost implications of the technology or the need for its regulation are not yet part of public discourse in India. The sensitive conversation around remote care here is still focused mainly on data and patient privacy. But home care is not something only the elderly need, nor is home-based care all about the latest technologies. Any patient who has undergone complicated treatment needs specialised care. Much like how some doctors insist on a particular pathological laboratory for diagnostic tests, they will also refer their patients to specific home-service providers and ask them to use only those providers.

Amita Sen recalls the time when her mother-in-law underwent an orthopaedic surgery at a prominent private hospital in Kolkata and developed some complications. She says that even before those problems had been resolved and their concerns addressed, the surgeon had already lined up a bunch of service providers and vendors to visit their home for physiotherapy, to change the dressings and to adjust the height of the toilet seat so that the convalescent could use it. 'We did not even have a choice in the matter and were expected to pay whatever charges they quoted,' she claims. 'We did not want to irk the doctor so we went with the providers he suggested.' When the designated professionals visited, the family realised that the same group of people worked with all of that doctor's patients.

7

Emergencies Feed Bottom Lines

There is an ad for a hospital that repeatedly plays on a Bengali news channel, showing an old man suffering what looks like a cardiac arrest in the middle of the night. The ad pitches a particular hospital which has a specific cardiac diagnostic equipment as the destination that can work miracles in such a dire situation. It ostensibly leverages state of the art medical equipment to attract potential customers, but the real currency in it is the helplessness that a family feels when faced with a sudden medical emergency. This pitch has been perfected for years and not just on screen.

Medical emergencies are among the primary drivers of medical inflation, where some of the individual money spinners for private hospitals such as 24/7 monitoring and testing overdrive organically coalesce. The very nature of an emergency means that very few questions can be asked about the clinical choices made on the spot, either by the patient's family or by doctors. When there is a sudden onset of illness and the diagnosis is unknown, there is an immediate need to not just find out the cause but also make sure that treating doctors know about the medical history of the patient as much as possible; if that is not possible by talking to the patient or their family members, as can happen in case of a road traffic accident, tests are the only option doctors have to get additional information about the patient. More tests therefore are carried out during an emergency than in a regular consultation and the bill skyrockets.

In March 2024, Arzoo Kumar was rushed to Fortis Hospital in Kolkata with acute back pain. She was advised admission and the hospital told her family that they had applied for pre-authorisation with their insurance company. She spent two nights and three days in hospital and was handed a bill of ₹1,20,209.77, of which ₹93,316 was only for investigative tests. The family had not given too much thought to what tests were being done or the rationale behind those decisions as the hospital had given them the impression that everything would be covered by insurance.

However, at the time of discharge, Arzoo's family was told that the insurer had denied the claim. The TPA for the insurer had evaluated the claim and issued the statement: 'Hospitalisation for evaluation and observation purposes. No active line of treatment, hence claim repudiated.' Her discharge summary had said that the patient was evaluated clinically as well as with relevant investigations. Her blood reports showed low levels of Vitamin D3. The ultrasound revealed that her left ovary had a cyst and her urinary bladder wall was thickened. The report of contrast enhanced computed tomography (CECT) of the whole abdomen was awaited. A magnetic resonance imaging (MRI) of the spine suggested sacroiliitis (inflammation of the joint where the spine connects to the pelvis) while reports were still pending at the time of discharge for a test for autoimmune markers. She had been treated conservatively as per the summary.[1]

The number of tests that Arzoo underwent is illustrative of what commonly happens in an emergency. She had undergone clinical investigation, blood and urine tests, an ultrasound, a CT scan, an MRI and even tests for autoimmune diseases but nothing concrete had been revealed about what caused the pain. The matter was referred to the insurance ombudsman. In the meantime, the West Bengal Clinical Establishment Regulatory Commission ruled that should the ombudsman uphold the decision of the insurer to reject the claim, the hospital would have to reduce the bill by ₹1 lakh as it concurred with the insurer that no treatment had been given, and it did not seem fair for the hospital to present a bill of ₹1.20 lakh for just trying to find out what had happened but giving no answers.

Cases like this in which a patient has contested a hospital bill and won are rare, because not many families have the time, energy and tenacity to pursue a case against a hospital once the patient has recovered and is back home. Post facto litigation is more common in cases of negligence in which the patient dies or is left disabled. Instances of emergency patients coming back with reams of test reports but without an actual course of treatment or an explanation of what triggered the emergency are common.

In an emergency, the 'uncertainty' that Kenneth Arrow writes about in his seminal treatise 'Uncertainty and the Welfare Economics of Medical Care'[2] presents itself in an aggravated form. A sudden unknown illness has struck and nobody, including the doctor sometimes, is certain what will work to alleviate the patient's suffering. This uncertainty leaves the sick person or their family – who are in this case the buyers of a service – powerless in any transaction with healthcare providers – who wield the power of the information (medical training and experience) they possess, not only to provide succour but also to drive the decisions in the transaction in any direction they desire. That could be in the direction of disinterested well-being of the patient; it can also be something that is beneficial for them or their institution.

Saheli Sen, a resident of Gurugram, suffered from a history of seizures since she was a child. But good care and regular medication had helped her lead a largely seizure-free life. However, the seizures returned one night. First one, then another with decreasing gap between two successive convulsions, until a time came when one seizure was barely over before Saheli collapsed into the next one. The duration of each seizure too increased as the night progressed. By the time her husband rushed her to a multispecialty hospital, the duration was close to two minutes. The doctor in the emergency ward gave her some medications, and to her husband's relief, Saheli responded positively. The seizures stopped.

Though she was feeling very weak and tired, the doctors at the hospital started her on a battery of pathological tests and imaging diagnostics. To the repeated queries about whether she had skipped her medicines, Saheli responded with a firm 'no'. However, the doctors insisted that she stay in the ICU so that she could be 'under constant monitoring'. By this time, she had been seizure-free for a few hours so the family did not quite understand why that was necessary. When they pressed an attending doctor on the matter, the reply stunned them: 'The administration has decided that she needs to be in the ICU.' Already anxious about Saheli's condition, the family refrained from arguing that ICU stay is a clinical not an administrative call.

Saheli remained in the ICU overnight and then was transferred to a regular single room for another night before being discharged on the third day. The doctor had insisted that she spend more time in the hospital as she still needed to be under observation, but the family decided against it. The bill for the two nights came to ₹1.18 lakh, which included laboratory charges and medical consumable charges of over ₹25,000 each. The room rent was ₹12,500, visiting consultant charges were ₹11,100 and pharmacy charges came to ₹8,000. The critical care charges exceeded ₹4,000, of which ₹1,100 was charged just for the insertion of a catheter.

Included in the list of medicines was an injectable paracetamol billed at ₹725 per unit. The oral version of the drug is available for as little as ₹20 per strip of ten tablets. The family was flummoxed, because at no point during her illness was Saheli in a state in which they could not administer medications orally. When a patient is in a critical state and there is an urgency for the medicine to start showing results, injectables are preferred as there may be concerns about the quality of oral medicines. But whether that was the reason for using the significantly more expensive option in Saheli's case was never explained to her or her husband.

Her family had many questions that doctors should ideally have answered. Beyond meeting their immediate requirement of stopping the seizures, the hospital did not even offer a cause for why the seizures happened, or a long-term plan to prevent them from recurring. 'We are not even sure whether they wanted us to prolong the stay for medical reasons or that again was an "administrative" decision,' says a relative. 'And why would the hospital administration have a say in which patients need to be in the ICU?' Her husband came back with the impression that the hospital was 'at a complete loss' on the clinical assessment and the doctors that took care of her were remarkably poor communicators. 'They were not even certain whether the interventions they had made would work. It almost seemed like a lucky chance that they did,' the relative told me. The family's health insurance paid for the hospitalisation and treatment but their doubts about the quality and competence of care persist. They are now thinking of seeking a second opinion for better clarity on what happened that night and how to prevent it in the future. Medical emergencies are trying times, so much so that not just laypeople but even doctors can find themselves at the receiving end of the tortuous and expensive private hospital processes.

Dr Achala Srivastava works for a top corporate hospital, so when her mother suddenly took ill with a severe headache, that hospital was the obvious choice for her. Her mother had a long history of high blood pressure and was immediately admitted to the hospital. After a while, Achala noticed that her mother seemed to have problems with comprehension and memory. At times, she came across as borderline delusional. As per protocol, the blood and urine samples were sent for routine diagnostic tests while a CT scan, MRI and venogram were performed.

CT scan uses X-rays to build 3D images of internal organs, an MRI on the other hand shows internal organs (both soft and hard tissues) with much more clarity. A venogram uses dye to check the health of blood vessels in the body.

It was found that Mrs Srivastava's sodium levels were lower than normal. However, the conclusion from all the tests was that the headache was linked to her high blood pressure at 220/120 mm Hg, which had been detected right at the time of admission. But the doctors declared that other causes had to be ruled out at her age, and hence all the other tests were essential. She was discharged after a couple of days. The bill was close to ₹1.5 lakh even after staff discount was applied. It was covered by health insurance.

A senior doctor who was involved with Mrs Srivastava's care explains that in an emergency, the correct course of action may not be obvious. 'There is a lot of clinical discretion involved, but a doctor cannot be faulted for being extra cautious,' he claims. Sometimes, doctors will approach a patient with certain preconceived notions, in which case they might order fewer tests. However, should that first impression be incorrect, such an approach might impede the process of reaching an accurate diagnosis and therefore delay appropriate treatment. In Mrs Srivastava's case, the doctors assumed that the patient had had a stroke. 'However, some discretion could still have been used,' admits the doctor. 'If the headache was due to a haemorrhagic stroke (when the breakage of a blood vessel in the brain cuts off supply to one part of it), it would have been visible in the CT scan. But instead several MRIs were done to find a clot that might have triggered the stroke. What might have clouded judgements is that she was showing symptoms of two problems – electrolyte imbalance that caused the confusion and the sudden rise in blood pressure that might have triggered the headache.'

In an emergency, a patient would be fortunate to simply get a straightforward diagnosis that can be clinically managed. Those who are advised surgery can have a stratospheric bill, because they undergo three independent cycles of healthcare inflation – the charges of the emergency drill, surgery-related expenses and then post-surgery referrals if required.

Global phenomenon

Much as India's healthcare is plagued by underfunding by the government and a regulatory vacuum, inflationary trends in emergency medicine transcend borders. In 2017, researchers from Johns Hopkins School of Medicine analysed Medicare billing records of 2,707 hospitals in the US and concluded that patients were routinely overcharged in an emergency. After looking at

12,337 emergency medicine bills, they calculated that there was a 340 per cent excess charge when a patient was admitted in an emergency compared to when they got planned care in the internal medicine department.[3]

A study by the University of Maryland School of Medicine looked at patients who were brought to the emergency ward and then admitted to the internal medicine department of a tertiary care medical centre and a hospital for military veterans in the USA. After reviewing the patients' charts, the study estimated that about a third of the tests ordered on the first day of hospitalisation were unnecessary. The most commonly ordered tests were chemistry 7 panel (which is a basic blood test that estimates blood electrolytes, glucose and various other metabolite levels in blood), complete blood count, prothrombin time (PT)/partial thromboplastin time (PTT), electrocardiogram and liver function test. The most commonly administered tests were PT/PTT, LFTs, urinalysis, the researchers concluded in their findings published in the *American Journal of Medicine* in 2021.[4]

Complete blood count looks at the various component cells of the blood (red cells, white cells, platelets) to look for infection or any blood disorders; PT and PTT are estimates of the clotting time of blood. In cases of extreme damage to the liver (such as poisoning), TPT and PTT readings may be abnormal, along with the results of the LFT. A lactate test measures the amount of lactic acid in blood. High levels of lactate can indicate a number of medical conditions, including tissue hypoxia (oxygen deprivation), shock, sepsis, heart failure, liver disease or certain metabolic disorders. In a standard corporate hospital in India, these tests could cost anything between ₹4,000 to ₹10,000. This amount can be daunting if the eventual treatment plan is not contingent upon these results.

Admittedly, American research results cannot be used to accurately assess the Indian healthcare system. But such analysis is hard to come by in our country. Doctors have occasionally spoken and written about the complex interplay of factors and vested interests that makes for pricey private healthcare. But it is not easy to find an academic assessment of the extent of excessive testing and overmedication in the private sector in India. This could be because given the reluctance hospitals have in sharing such data, the full extent of the problem can only be estimated by an insider. Most doctors who are a part of the private system are understandably not keen to take on their employers.

An oncologist based out of Bihar once told me that doctors are not responsible for the billing practices of the hospitals they work at, nor are their inputs sought on the matter. 'But if you ask my personal opinion, if a person chooses to stay in a single room, that person can be charged a little extra.' The 'extra' can vary widely from test to test. For example, a routine stool and microscopy test for which a patient would be charged about ₹500 in a hospital could be done for less than ₹150 at a standard pathological laboratory. A stool culture and sensitivity test, which looks at the kind of organism that is involved in a gastrointestinal infection, costs around ₹800 at a pathological laboratory not attached to any hospital. In a corporate hospital it can cost more than double that amount.

In the media, as in academic journals, the scrutiny is reserved largely for the public sector or occasionally for the unorganised private sector that fills in the gaps in Tier II and Tier III cities. If one believes the coverage in mainstream media, then corporate hospitals in India are the next-generation healthcare destinations where complicated surgeries are done with state-of-the-art equipment, sometimes on foreign nationals who are given new leases of life. There is some truth in projecting private hospitals as beacons of cutting-edge medical practice, but that is not the whole truth. The primary reason for this positive representation in the mainstream media is that the private healthcare sector is a source of significant advertising revenue. Thus, while both minor and major slipups in government hospitals may be highlighted, coverage of the private sector is largely laudatory in nature. Many media houses hold marquee award events or summits with multiple sponsors. Sometimes these events are focussed solely on healthcare and various private hospitals are presented with awards under diverse categories. Many of the awardee hospitals may also feature on the sponsors' list for the same event.

The scrutiny of the government sector though is far from unjustified. The Constitution of India mandates public health as a duty of the state. While the adverse implications of privatisation in a sellers' market such as healthcare have been discussed at great length for decades, the truth is that the growth and unfettered proliferation of the private sector in India stems from the public sector not fulfilling its duties – first, to ensure the health and nutrition (as stated in the Constitution) of its citizens and second, to regulate private healthcare.

Every few years, the National List of Essential Medicines (NLEM) is revised to account for the changing landscape of medicine and healthcare. All drugs included in the list automatically come under price control, which means that their MRPs are capped by the government. The capped price is based on the prices of the highest-selling brands of these medicines in the market. Then in 2018, the government of India started discussions on capping prices of 'essential' diagnostic tests, in line with the approach adopted for drugs. The Indian Council of Medical Research (ICMR) then released a list of essential diagnostic tests that had to be available at various levels of healthcare facilities such as primary health centres, community health centres and district hospitals.

This kind of list, with detailed testing guidelines about essential and optional tests, could somewhat ease the problem of unnecessary tests being prescribed in emergencies. However, unlike the NLEM, there were no limits nor recommendations on pricing associated with this list. ICMR has now released a revised list,[5] but the hopes of price guidelines being added remain unfulfilled. It will not be easy to implement price caps on diagnostic tests given the collective might of the Indian corporate hospital and diagnostics lab behemoths.

Profiteering by private hospitals had faced some government scrutiny during the COVID-19 pandemic. Regardless, many of these hospitals treated the humanitarian crisis as a peerless business opportunity to be milked to the maximum. There were instances when emergency patients were falsely declared as positive for the

SARS-CoV-2 virus, and their families charged for the thoroughly overpriced and – as was later proved – useless drug Remdesivir.

After one such instance, a police complaint was lodged against a private hospital in Panchkula. Tarsem Chand was taken to the emergency room with chest pains in January 2022, during the third wave of COVID-19 in India. The hospital found he tested positive for COVID-19. This meant that the family was no longer able to meet him, and Chand was left completely at the mercy of the hospital. After he had been taken to the COVID-19 ward, the family was told that he had suffered a cardiac arrest. As per the extant law, all COVID-19 cases had to be mandatorily reported to the government. So, Chand's son filed an RTI application and found out that there was no record with the government of Chand ever having had COVID-19. The RTI reply was the basis on which the police registered his complaint.[6]

Unfortunately, RTI is applicable only to publicly funded organisations and is not useful in exposing malpractices by private hospitals, which do not come under the Act. The only recourse available is to approach consumer courts or state consumer commissions. But very few patients or their families exercise these options.

Nascent specialty

It was only in 2009 that emergency medicine first entered the medical college curriculum in India as an academic discipline. However, the doctors who have been the pioneers of this specialty in the country concede that in practice this department at various colleges remains understaffed, sometimes run by personnel filling in from other departments. This ad hocism often stands in the way of quality patient care and by extension to the costs incurred for treatment during emergencies. There are no universal protocols for emergency care in India and the staff posted in emergency wards are often inexperienced, with inadequate clinical judgement.

In 2020, AIIMS released a report on emergency and injury care in secondary and tertiary care centres in the country.[7] They looked at emergency and trauma care services of 100 such hospitals in 29 states and two union territories from five regions of India to assess the state of care and the challenges in the sector. The report reveals that typically most of the 'emergency care' in Indian hospitals is provided in areas known as 'Casualty' or 'Accident'. Formal education and specialty training in emergency care are neither available nor mandatory for personnel involved in emergency care. These Causality/Accident room physicians lack any specific training in emergency medicine.

'Residents posted in these "rooms" often rotate from various specialties such as surgery, orthopaedics and medicine and have little commitment towards patient management,' states the report. 'These physicians are often waiting to retake the All-India Entrance Examination in the hope of securing a postgraduate position in established fields.' In some hospitals, emergency rooms are divided into separately administered medical and surgical teams: 'With this division it becomes very difficult to deliver quality, cost-effective care. In many hospitals, physicians staffing the emergency rooms lack the resources and knowledge to manage the wide variety of emergencies.' The report likens them to 'postal workers' who 'deliver' victims of accidents to various specialties. 'The most junior and inexperienced staff frequently treat the most seriously injured patients,' the report laments.

The study found that satisfaction levels are usually higher at private hospitals than at public sector institutions but did not delve into the matter of price regulation. Among the other revealing statistics in the report, it was found that 41 per cent of hospitals had a documented emergency manual, 30 per cent had documented policies and procedures for patient transfers, 57 per cent gave a discharge summary to patients, 58 per cent had policies on handling patient deaths, 44 per cent hospitals had documented disaster management plans and only 41 per cent had a triage policy.

Besides the fact that a vast majority of hospitals had no emergency manual nor documented policies for patient transfer, it was remarkable that over 40 per cent did not give a discharge summary to a patient. A discharge summary has a summary of the patient's diagnosis, their treatment and the future course of action to be undertaken. Not only is it an important document for any physician the patient may consult next, but it is also a mandatory requirement to ensure continuity in medical care. Wherever the patient goes for treatment later, the doctors there should be able to easily access the patient's history and medical records.

Documented policies and procedures for patient transfer are also important to ensure that hospitals do not transfer out critical patients so that their own records look good, while triage policies are important in an emergency department for when there are large-scale casualties, such as in a disaster, as it ensures that the most critical patients get attended to first. Lack of a triage policy can cause confusion and chaos particularly when the emergency ward is supervised by inexperienced doctors, as is often the case in India. According to a senior professor in an apex government trauma centre, emergency manuals are very important for providing quality, standardised emergency care.

A top neurosurgeon at a government tertiary care institute says that all the protocols are clearly laid out where he works. 'I do not know if private sector hospitals have that [clear protocols] but in the way they practise their medicine, there are a lot of deviations from established clinical norms,' he says. 'For example, for patients with a head injury, the first test of choice is always a CT scan. It takes about a minute and may cost around ₹1,000 in a private hospital. But among such patients from the private sector that I have seen, most have undergone an MRI but not a CT scan. An MRI takes about 30 minutes and can cost anything between ₹10,000 and ₹30,000. There is no reason to do it instead of a CT scan but private hospitals do that very frequently.'

In India, if a patient is brought to a hospital after a road accident or in an emergency, the hospital is bound by law to treat the patient at least until they are in a position to be moved to another hospital. This applies to all hospitals, whether government or private, irrespective of whether the patient has the means to pay. If the patient can afford to remain in the private hospital, they may stay until they recover. But if not, they may choose to shift to a government-run trauma centre. The neurosurgeon complains about the lack of uniformity in discharge norms at private hospitals. 'There is a metric called the Glasgow Coma Scale that is used to measure consciousness in a patient with head trauma,' he explains. 'Often the discharge summary from a private hospital does not even mention that. Thus, I must conduct my own assessment and tests, duplicating efforts and losing precious treatment time.'

In private hospitals, the ordeal for patients usually starts only when it is time to pay. But sometimes it can start earlier, particularly in the emergency ward. Asmita Mahanta recounts the time when her mother had to be rushed to a private hospital with respiratory distress. 'I was anxious. My father was in a different city and my mother had been suffering all evening. The doctor in the emergency ward was polite and very solicitous,' she says, adding that it calmed her nerves a bit … until she saw him writing the prescription while checking dosages on the internet on his smartphone! These encounters are not conducive to building trust in the doctor–patient relationship. Every few days, a doctor in India is manhandled by the disgruntled relatives of patients. A vast majority of these attacks happen in the emergency department when emotions run high.

Tempers get frayed not just because of the uncertainties of an emergency room but also the lack of accountability. Journalist Rekha Vats recalls the time she had to rush her son to a top Gurgaon hospital with excruciating stomach pain. An ultrasound was done and some fluids administered in the emergency ward. After a while, a nurse came and told her that the ultrasound report was not clear so they would need to come back the next day and do another one. 'Then they charged me ₹13,000,' she says. 'I could not understand what the charges were for. A couple of bottles of fluids could not cost that much and the ultrasound was inconclusive. What is a test without a report! But when we went back the next day and did the ultrasound again, they charged us a second time for the same test.'

Adoption of unsuitable international guidelines for emergency care has added to the challenges of delivering affordable care. A Delhi-based internist at a trust hospital cites the example of the antibiotic test dose, which he says only needs to be administered when the patient has a history of allergy to that particular class of drugs. 'But now doctors have started doing that test routinely in emergencies,' says the internist. 'That is a guideline for an accountable, publicly funded health system.' He says that it doesn't make any sense to apply that guideline in India, where there is no such system.

An antibiotic test dose is a small amount of the prescribed antibiotic administered to the patient to check for any untoward allergic reactions to the medicine. The test dose is usually less than the actual dose and for some medicines, multiple test doses of increasing quantity are used before starting the actual course of treatment. While the cost implications of this practice are not much, a test may prolong the stay in the hospital as the patient's response to the drug is monitored. This extended stay can increase the hospital bill.

Doctors from the NH Rabindranath Tagore International Institute of Cardiac Sciences, Kolkata, published an article in 2019 in the *Journal of the Association of Physicians of India* about the practice of skin testing prior to administration of antibiotics.[8] They emphasise that the practice, in the absence of a history of allergy, is unheard of in the medical literature of the West. They also claim that the practice of giving a test dose prior to administration of an antibiotic has no scientific basis.

Despite this, in both government and private hospitals and nursing homes in India, skin testing prior to administration of antibiotics remains extremely common and is even considered to be negligence if not done. The article says that based on the evidence available, skin testing should be restricted to patients with a history of prior penicillin allergy, for whom penicillin or other B-lactam antibiotic is the drug of choice and there is no suitable alternative. 'There is no need to do skin testing without a history of penicillin allergy even if the drug is to be administered parenterally,' the article suggests. 'Test dose administration does not protect patients from anaphylactic reactions, and hence the practice has no scientific basis.'

8

'Do You Have Insurance?'

'Do you know the first question you are asked when you walk in as an outpatient?' A specialist who has just moved out of one of eastern India's biggest corporate hospital chains poses the question. He is talking about the reasons for the shift and the question is about his successor's OPD. He then offers the answer: 'Do you have insurance?' He then bursts out laughing and asks why a patient who has just walked into the clinic should be asked about insurance, given that there has been no discussion about hospitalisation as yet. He provides the explanation without being prompted. 'It is because if a person has insurance, they will be much more malleable and open to doing more expensive diagnostic tests and to even the suggestion of spending a night at the hospital for a thorough check-up.'

Doctors are often asked by their hospitals why they are not admitting a larger number of patients despite seeing hundreds of them every day in their clinics. For hospitals, the bread and butter of their existence are the inpatients, with OPD being mainly seen as a robust 'supply chain' for admissions. Sometimes a new doctor who has just joined a hospital will candidly explain to the patient that while their condition does not necessitate admission, the recommendation is so that their diagnostic tests are paid for by the insurance company. A person with health insurance is less concerned about expenses, because they are not paying out of pocket. Moreover there is an element of rudimentary price regulation for policyholders since many hospitals also offer lower rates for patients with insurance – as per their agreement with the provider companies.

A big salary package for the doctor, meanwhile, is a relatively new but increasingly pervasive factor in the private hospital ecosystem, marking a significant shift in the healthcare model. At the dawn of private healthcare in India, when the East India Company set up a hospital in Fort St George in Madrasapatnam in 1664, the doctors and the trust that patients had in both their skill and their integrity have been the mainstays of the healthcare business. *Healer*, the biography of Dr Prathap C. Reddy, by Pranay Gupte paints a candid picture of how Apollo Hospitals built its reputation with renowned names in oncology both from India and abroad such as Dr Vijay Anand Reddy, Dr Harsh Dua, Dr Umanath Nayak, Dr S.V.S.S. Prasad and Dr Jonas Stumpf from Budapest, who was roped in to operate the high dose Selectron – a radiation machine – and continued with Apollo for several years afterwards. A famous doctor added to the prestige of a hospital and brought in patients. Sometimes the patients would change hospitals too if the doctor switched jobs.

A pulmonary medicine doctor who has worked at a private hospital for 23 years claims that he has never taken any salary from the hospital. 'In fact, I used to pay 10 per cent of my fees to the hospital,' he says. 'That gave me the freedom to practise my medicine with integrity.' He says that when the management asked him about the low admission rate, he dismissed them half-jestingly: 'I am a good doctor, so I can heal patients just in the OPD.' There would be occasional queries about why he was prescribing so few tests, and he would tell them he used his own professional discretion to analyse patients and would not just have tests done because somebody wanted him to. If the conversation got any more intense, the doctor could counter the mounting pressure by reminding them that they did not pay him a salary. In fact, it was he who paid them a part of his earnings, in return for using their facilities to see patients, so he would continue to rely on his own clinical judgement rather than give in to extraneous considerations. 'Hospitals have now understood the flaw in that system,' he says. 'Hence the advent of the salaried consultant doctor who is beholden to the hospital and has no choice but to prescribe as many diagnostic tests and admit as many patients as his "targets" demand.' For these salaried employees, the patient's insurance status is almost as important as their vital signs.

The number of doctors on monthly salaries are steadily increasing as corporate hospitals work on further diluting the doctor–patient relationship by making the doctor faceless and nameless. It is the hospital that the patient goes to. In Vellore, for example, a patient may go to Shankar Nethralaya, but they rarely ever look to consult a specific doctor there. They place their trust in the institution rather than the individual. 'That is the model that private hospitals now want to emulate to shift the power dynamic within the system,' says a senior doctor who has lived the transition. The effort is to subtly shift the pivot from the doctor's personal fame to the reputation of the hospital. Corporate hospitals continue to advertise 'acquisitions' of reputed senior consultants but most of the younger doctors are on a monthly retainership.

A Kolkata-based anaesthesiologist, who is not affiliated to any hospital, explains to me how the decision-making gears in corporate hospitals have gradually moved from the clinician or surgeon to a cadre of employees who specialise in business and finance and are adept at reading balance sheets but not necessarily MRIs and CT scans. 'There is no right or wrong in this,' he says. 'In fact, with the government not fulfilling its responsibility of ensuring quality healthcare for the people, the private sector has become the only option for a large proportion of the population.' Private hospitals have costs – the infrastructure, equipment, utilities and staff salaries – that need to be covered. 'Businesses need to sustain themselves, so the CEOs of every big hospital now are people from a non-medical, business background,' he continues. 'It is inevitable that they will ask doctors who are employees to do things that are in the interest of the hospital over that of the patient.'

In recent years, the Indian healthcare industry has emerged as a destination for multinational investors looking for quick and safe returns. Singapore-based investment firm Tamasek acquired a stake in the Manipal Hospital Group recently,[1] while Apollo Hospitals has tied up with another Singapore-based entity called the Parkway Group for establishing the Apollo Gleneagles Hospital in Kolkata.[2] Malaysian fund Khazanah too has been sporadically investing in Indian healthcare. Many doctors feel that this set of new entrants have also changed the healthcare business, bringing in a sharper focus on the profitability benchmark and bringing in more cutting-edge professional approaches to the way hospitals are run, maximizing resource and manpower utilisation. The infusion of funds has also helped Indian hospitals access the latest medical technology, making them preferred destinations for patients from around the world, not just within the country.

Another senior doctor, who has been in practice for over three decades and seen this transition firsthand, elaborates: 'We see a trend now of multinational investors and companies increasingly adding Indian healthcare companies to their "portfolio". The raison d'etre of these companies is returns on their investments so safeguards are being put at all levels to secure that. This is where the senior management comes in, to ensure facilities are used and monetised to the maximum extent possible.'

'Testing' times

While there is a lot of medical literature available about the overuse of diagnostic tests in hospitalised patients,[3] most of these studies were unfortunately not done in India. There is no analysis about whether patients with health insurance are subjected to more tests than those without, but anecdotally, that does seem to be the case. This is because despite the insurance companies' intense scrutiny of the hospital bills, there is enough room for clinical discretion for some additional tests to be slipped in.

The insurers cannot deny payment for those tests as they could be medically justified. Some such tests that are commonly overused internationally are the echocardiography, endoscopy and colonoscopy.[4]

A resident doctor at a Delhi hospital, who has had the experience of working with several different departments, explains, 'Screening tests are often overused, particularly in elderly patients. A doctor who has not had a clear diagnosis for a patient with gastrointestinal problems may ask for an endoscopy or a colonoscopy more readily when they know that the extra charges would be covered by insurance,' he reveals. 'And they have a perfectly legitimate reason to do so. This is also true for prostate screenings or urine culture tests. It is very difficult for anybody who is not a clinician and has not faced exactly the same situation in an identical patient to decide whether the tests were required or not.' A Mumbai-based gastrointestinal surgeon says that his colleagues 'have an obsession with the orifices of the human body and regularly recommend invasive procedures such as endoscopy and colonoscopy. I call it orificeology – this obsession doctors have with the orifices of the human body. You probably do not know of any person without some GI [gastrointestinal] symptoms. These are the perfect candidates for endoscopy.' Either procedure could cost over ₹5,000 at a private hospital.

There are many such discretionary tests. In some cases medical device companies incentivise the uptake of tests by marking up the prices of consumables so that hospitals can also keep a margin there in addition to the price of the test. An internal medicine consultant uses the example of a machine that can be used for point of care tests in cases of cardiac arrest or pulmonary embolism to illustrate this. It can measure the level of a protein called troponin in the blood and reveals if the patient has had a cardiac event and how recently it may have occurred. It can also perform the D-dimer test for blood clots and is very good for diagnostic purposes if used for the right patient.

'The machine costs about ₹2.5 lakh to ₹3 lakh and a single-use kit is priced at ₹2,100, but the hospital charges ₹9,000 for the test,' reveals the consultant. 'If a patient has insurance, he is more amenable to undergoing the test. The cost of the machine can be recovered several times over within a year. For a doctor who is not mindful of the patient's bill – or if he is actively looking to raise it to meet the targets set by management – this test is prone to overuse.'

Another commonly overprescribed test in surgical patients is viral serology, which looks at infections such as hepatitis A, hepatitis B and HIV (human immunodeficiency virus). Hospitals say that the test needs to be done to protect the OT staff against inadvertent infection that can happen if somebody accidentally pricks themselves during the surgery. The test costs anything between ₹1,500 to ₹2,000, and is 'one of the most useless tests' in the opinion of a Delhi-based surgeon working at a top hospital. 'There is no justification for doing it for a patient without any history of risky behaviour or symptoms that may warrant this test. Laboratories make millions from this totally unnecessary test,' he declares. His opinion is that because these infections pop up about once in six months, the risk is not that high. Another aspect of the corporate hospital's business model is that the ones with a laboratory will insist on all tests being done in-house, claiming that all others are prone to inaccuracies. If there is no laboratory then samples will usually be sent to pathlabs with which there is a prior understanding. 'Some hospitals continue to do COVID-19 tests – again, without any medical justification,' says the surgeon. With the infection making a transient and fortunately feeble comeback in the summer of 2025, this practice may have got an additional lease of life.

Preventive HIV testing has now been normalised by corporate hospitals to the extent that it is no longer questioned.

In the decades since the unravelling of the structure of the DNA in 1953, technologies such as polymerase chain reaction – widely used for the detection of the SARS-CoV-2 virus during the COVID-19 pandemic but also well established as a cutting-edge diagnostic technique from much earlier – and advancements in microscopy have established the importance of modern technology in medical diagnosis.[5] However, the importance of physicians remains paramount, as it is their clinical acumen and balanced decision-making that are key to the optimum usage of all diagnostic techniques. Used correctly, they can revolutionise patient care. But they can equally well become tools to increase healthcare costs, should doctors shun conscientious decision-making.

The pulmonary medicine consultant mentions a 'fantastic' PCR-based test that can analyse sputum or lower respiratory tract samples from a patient with a lung ailment and identify the nature of the organism from among 22 viruses and 17 bacteria. This is a boon particularly for unconscious patients on ventilators. But at ₹25,000 per test, it can put unnecessary financial stress on a patient if it is not actually required. The test only costs about ₹16,000 to the hospital, so the markup is significant. It is down to the doctor to choose between clinical and business interests when prescribing the test; in an insured patient the moral dilemma is of course far less.

Another 'bread and butter' test is the fever panel test, which involves several blood and urine tests such as complete blood count (an assessment of all the different types of blood cells), liver and kidney function tests and also a malaria test in some cases. At a pathological laboratory it can cost ₹600 to ₹1,200, but at a corporate hospital, a patient would be charged ₹2,000 to ₹5,000 for that same test. Almost all inpatients undergo this test, but how many of them really need it? Answers are hard to find. There are similar 'panel tests' for diarrhoea, respiratory issues and meningitis, among others, which have replaced disease-specific tests. In the absence of universal and mandatory standard treatment guidelines or an honest prescription audit undertaken either by hospitals or by authorities with the mandate to do so, there is no way to assess the extent of overprescription of diagnostic tests.

Over the last two decades, the central government has been trying to increase medical manpower after successive estimations by the World Health Organisation (WHO) have found India far below par on that parameter. In 2022, the government of India told the Rajya Sabha that at 1:834, India's doctor-to-population ratio is better than 1:1000 as prescribed by WHO.[6] However, this calculation included alternative medicine practitioners commonly clubbed as AYUSH (which stands for Ayurveda, Yoga, Unani, Siddha and Homoeopathy), which is not the global norm. Besides, there are deep structural and regulatory issues in alternative medicine, including concerns about quality of drugs and standards of training.

However, the overwhelming focus on sheer numbers of doctors produced every year has led to quality suffering for the sake of quantity. Tales of inspection teams encountering fake patients and professors in medical colleges are so common that the National Medical Commission recently released guidelines to identify such fakes.[7] It has also led to medical education in the country becoming prohibitively expensive. Both these factors add to the conditions in which the cost of medical care increases. Compromising on the quality of medical education means that new medical graduates have poorer clinical sense, which makes their professional judgement hostage to a large number of tests. On the other hand, their expensive education makes them willing accomplices in corporate profiteering. With huge student loans to pay off, these newly minted medical graduates are more likely to prescribe extra tests to meet the demands of their employers than perhaps the previous generation of doctors.

The government's focus on increasing the number of medical colleges has resulted in a mushrooming of these institutes, some with minimal facilities and others with high fees. In 2023, D.Y. Patil Medical College in Navi Mumbai was reported to charge ₹1.3 crore for a bachelor's degree in medicine.[8] While that may be an outlier, the cost of a medical degree from a private medical college could easily exceed ₹50 lakh on average. This is a significant shift from the days when students of medicine could get a highly subsidised education at a government medical college and then slowly build a practice. Seats were fewer and competition was fierce, unlike now when virtually anybody who studies bioscience at the plus two level can get enrolled in a medical college. Thousands of medical graduates being churned out every year form a willing pool of candidates for the new-age hiring model of private hospitals – that of salaried doctors.

A senior doctor at a government hospital in Delhi cites the example of a dengue serology test, which would cost somewhere between ₹600 and ₹1,000 at a pathology lab and double that amount for an inpatient in a private hospital. But is not essential for a treatment decision. In fact, this logic is often used during a dengue outbreak, to keep official numbers low. Dengue is a notifiable disease, every confirmed positive test must be reported to the government. During an outbreak, doctors at public institutes are sometimes informally instructed to reply more on symptomatic diagnosis to treat patients rather than report a large number of cases that might cause unnecessary panic. However in corporate hospitals, the patient's sample will, as a matter of routine, be sent for a fever panel and then for a battery of tests, including dengue and sundry other infections, significantly inflating the bill.

For the insured, this gamut of tests is not a concern, and that is why whether patients have health cover or not is an important question for corporate hospitals.

Defensive medicine

In June 2024, the National Consumer Disputes Redressal Forum fined a hospital in Kolkata ₹75 lakh for delay in diagnosis of post-bariatric surgery complications that resulted in the death of the patient.[9] It added ₹2 lakh in litigation expenses for the aggrieved party. A general medicine specialist and an anaesthetist were found to have delayed the process of diagnosis of the complications.

In February 2024, the Delhi State Consumer Disputes Redressal Forum fined Sir Ganga Ram Hospital over ₹7 lakh for the death of a woman who had been admitted to the hospital for a spleen surgery in 2015. In addition, the family of the woman received ₹90,000 in litigation costs.[10]

In 2009, the Supreme Court of India awarded Dr Kunal Saha, an Ohio-based HIV specialist, ₹20 lakh for the death of his wife, Anuradha Saha, in 1998. Anuradha had been given an excessive dose of a steroid while the two were in Kolkata on vacation. Four doctors and the Advanced Medicare Institute in Kolkata were found guilty of medical negligence.[11] This was a landmark judgement in the history of Indian medicine, one of the foundational cases in jurisprudence on medical negligence. But judgements such as these have, along with many other factors, also had an unforeseen effect. They have gradually changed the way medicine is practised in India, paving the way for defensive medicine. There is a surfeit of medical literature available about the practice in the US, but for India the challenge is that average income levels can barely support basic healthcare, and the low insurance penetration makes defensive medicine one of the top contributors to healthcare-related impoverishment of families.

A doctor practising in West Bengal recalls a case in Kolkata in which a doctor was found guilty of negligence because they had not done an ECG on a 24-year-old girl who subsequently died of a cardiac arrest on the surgical table. 'In such a case, a doctor would ordinarily exercise their own judgement,' he says. 'I too would not have done an ECG, because you do not expect a 24-year-old to have a heart condition. Every surgical procedure has a chance of mortality even if it is as low as 0.001 per cent. What this figure means is that somebody somewhere has died on the table; that's why it is not zero. But that is not the benchmark against which clinical decisions are taken. We have now started to prescribe tests instead of relying on our clinical judgement. This would, we understand, inflate the bill, but with the risk of a legal challenge looming, which doctor would not be cautious?'

In 2013, researchers at Manipal University published an article in *Annals of Medical and Health Science Research* listing casualties of defensive medicine, among which was the trust between doctor and patient.[12] Doctors in India have traditionally enjoyed deep respect and trust from society in general. To this day, when doctors introduce themselves in a gathering, they are greeted with immediate awe and veneration. The erosion of that trust is what has pushed patients and their families to knock on the doors of courts in the first place.

And because patients have started to question their decisions, doctors have taken to prescribing tests not for clinical reasons but out of fear of the hypothetical litigation they may have to face if they didn't take all precautions. This further erodes trust because patients feel that they are being subjected to tests that return no findings but add to their bill. Most physicians in top hospitals now purchase malpractice insurance as a safety net.

An article published in 2022 in the journal *Indian Pediatrics* lists the factors contributing to defensive medicine.[13] Among them are the need for certainty of the diagnosis, a lack of hierarchy in medical care, the exponential growth of micro/super specialisations and corporate health institutions. It also lists incentive-based practice, increasing incidences of violence against health personnel, the rising trend of defamation suits against doctors, bad publicity by the media and interference by elected representatives as reasons that have caused doctors to err on the side of caution.

But the knowledge that clinical decisions will not be assessed against a financial benchmark, can also mean reduced accountability for doctors treating insured patients. Sumana Roy, who is 80 years old and lives alone in a suburb in Kolkata, had a fall and fractured her hip joint. Mistaking it for a minor injury she was a little late in seeking medical attention but when she finally did, she was advised immediate admission. She had a generous government medical insurance and was admitted to a posh hospital in Kolkata. There, an X-ray confirmed the fracture, and she was wheeled in for a corrective surgery.

When she was admitted, she had a haemoglobin of 10.2. Keeping her age and medical history in mind, a referral was given to an internal medicine specialist, who looked at all the physiological parameters and confirmed that she had the cardiovascular fitness to undergo the procedure. After the surgery, her family was told that she would need blood. They were not told the reason for it, but reports showed that her haemoglobin had dropped to 6. This could mean only one thing – she had lost a lot of blood during the surgery – but no explanations were offered to her family. Over the next couple of days, four units of blood were pumped into her, taking the duration of hospitalisation beyond the three days initially anticipated. Just as the family was expecting her haemoglobin to rise enough to allow her to be discharged, Sumana went into heart failure.

The internal medicine specialist told the family that she was not in a state to be released because in that state she might rapidly deteriorate and may even need to be put on a ventilator. He also recorded his conversations with the patient and sent the videos to the family, who were naturally flustered by how unwell she seemed to be. He hinted that the chronic obstructive pulmonary disease that Sumana had been diagnosed with a few years earlier may have been a case of wrong diagnosis and insinuated that she had in fact been living with an undiagnosed heart problem. The family was distraught. She was finally released after a week. Her insurance cover meant the family did not have to worry about the bill even though the sudden complications and inadequate explanations left them dissatisfied with the quality of care. They were at a loss to understand what had really happened in the hospital and whether she had indeed developed a heart condition. However, Sumana's personal physician later told her that the heart failure may have been triggered by the rapid transfusion of blood post surgery and not because she had an underlying condition. He also said that it is a very common phenomenon after rapid infusion of blood and was surprised that the doctor went to such great lengths to give such a misleading impression.

Moral hazard

Recommending unnecessary or repetitive diagnostic procedures is not the only way that private hospitals inflate bills and bottom lines. When a certain sum of money is assured for the patient in the form of medical insurance, there is sometimes an unsaid urgency for hospitals to get as much of that corpus as possible. This is why there is a term in health insurance called 'moral hazard', which refers to the danger of doing some surgeries just because they will be paid for. Some of the top ones in this category are hysterectomy, caesarean sections and appendectomy. For all surgeries, patient consent is paramount so doctors can, if they want, take the position that the patient's keenness for that procedure was what spurred them.

Similar data on other common organs that may be removed without any significant disruption of bodily functions – such as the appendix and gallbladder – are harder to come by, but medical literature is replete with references to negative appendectomy, in which the appendix (a vestigial organ with no significant functions but which can be very painful and potentially fatal if infected) has been removed even when it is not infected.

Surgeons concede that negative appendectomies are often done in smaller medical centres on patients with access to insurance; the percentage of such patients has gone up in recent years with the coming of PMJAY and a bouquet of insurance programmes run by individual state governments. A Delhi-based gastrointestinal surgeon working at one of the top hospitals of the region says that more common than appendectomies are cholecystectomies for asymptomatic gallstones. 'In big cities these days, annual health check-ups have become very popular. A common, incidental ultrasound finding is of asymptomatic gallstones,' he explains. 'It is entirely up to the doctor whether they want to give honest advice to the patient – which would be to come back if they ever have pain – or talk them into a surgical procedure just because the person has insurance.'

The surgeon adds that while it can be a clinical call to recommend surgery, occasionally the doctors will simply tell the patient to get it removed before they develop pain and have to be rushed to the hospital in an emergency. They even frighten them with the warnings such as if left unremoved, it could lead to cancer. These are all factual statements but do not necessarily paint an accurate picture because not all gallstones will progress to these stages. A large number will remain asymptomatic for life. A cholecystectomy can cost an estimated ₹12 lakh in a private hospital. The cholecystectomy package under PMJAY, depending on whether it is availed in a Tier I, Tier II or Tier III city, ranges from ₹86,900 to ₹1,04,200.

However, doctors point out that some of the most commonly abused surgeries are gynaecological. The number of Caesarean sections that affluent women in urban centres undergo are several orders of magnitude higher than what happens in those with limited means in rural areas, when physiologically speaking, the percentage of C-secs in each category – urban areas and rural areas – should be comparable. A common refrain from obstetricians in Delhi's elite hospitals is that expectant mothers want Caesarean deliveries because they want the child to be born on a particular date of astrological significance or because they are unwilling to go through long and painful labour. However, there are reams of data to show that there is a positive and linear correlation between procedures such as caesarean sections and hysterectomies and the availability of insurance coverage.

India's caesarean section rate is far higher than the global average.[14]

The data on Caesarean section deliveries from the National Family Health Survey 5 – which is the latest available statistic – show that 32.3 per cent of the births in urban India and 17.6 per cent of births in rural India happen surgically.[15] This is much higher than the global average. The breakup of Caesarean sections between private and government facilities is revealing. Between 2019 and 2021 – the period covered by the survey – 49.3 per cent deliveries at private hospitals in urban India and 46 per cent deliveries at private hospitals in rural India were by Caesarean section. The corresponding figures for government health facilities were 22.7 per cent for urban centres and 11.9 per cent for rural establishments.

Patients going to private hospitals are more likely to have some form of health insurance than those going to government hospitals. A 2020 study that analysed Caesarean section deliveries in India found that people with health insurance had a higher likelihood of giving birth through surgical means.[16] Caesarean section delivery also happens to be among the top ten most used packages under PMJAY. How does India's Caesarean section rates compare to global averages? In 2018, WHO had developed programmatic guidance to reduce the rising rates of Caesarean sections across the world. Concomitant with this process, the reputed medical journal *The Lancet* had published an article titled 'Global Epidemiology of Use of and Disparities in Caesarean Sections' in which a rate of 10 per cent to 15 per cent was termed as 'optimal' for caesarean section deliveries.[17] Hysterectomy – in which the female reproductive organs are removed – is also more common in India than in the rest of the world. Studies have found that the rates are relatively higher in West and South India, where the healthcare infrastructure is better. A white paper released in 2023 by the Federation of Obstetric and Gynaecological Societies of India states that 3.3 per cent of Indian women have undergone a hysterectomy.[18] It is the most common non-obstetric gynaecological surgery amongst women of reproductive age. The paper also warns against unnecessary hysterectomies performed in cases where non-invasive treatment would have been sufficient. There are also reports of potential coercion for financial benefit under health insurance schemes and concerns about the lack of information provided to women about its side effects. Two-thirds of all hysterectomies (3.3 per cent according to National Family Health Survey 5) were carried out in the private sector. The document also references a working paper from the National Health Authority on early trends from PMJAY that indicates that of all claims submitted by or for women, 2 per cent were for hysterectomy. The states of Chhattisgarh, Uttar Pradesh, Jharkhand, Gujarat, Maharashtra and Karnataka had the highest number of claims under PMJAY and also generated three-quarters of all hysterectomy claims. The lack of both regulations as well as any meaningful adherence to standard treatment guidelines have also impacted insurance premiums in India. The result is a cycle of low insurance uptake and bankruptcy because of catastrophic health expenses. To offset the 'moral hazard' problem, PMJAY came up with the idea of reserving for government hospitals certain packages that may be overused. With the release of its latest list of health benefit packages, the National Health Authority issued guidelines stating that it was the discretion of the states to reserve packages for public hospitals based on their local conditions and availability of infrastructure. However, certain packages – such as those for hysterectomy, high-risk childbirth and mental health – were 'recommended' to be reserved for public sector hospitals.[19]

As it turned out, such measures were not enough to keep 'enterprising' hospitals from resorting to dubious schemes to boost profits. Angioplasties have very recently emerged as a 'moral hazard' procedure under PMJAY after the Khyati Multi-Speciality Hospital in Gujarat was accused of doing angioplasties on patients who had PMJAY coverage even when they did not need them. One of the patients was only 18 years old.[20] Under ordinary circumstances it is difficult for a non-medical person to assess whether an angioplasty was warranted or not, but the problem came to light when some of these patients died.[21]

A subsequent government inquiry found that at least seven patients' angioplasties had been done even when they were not needed. There were instances in which the blockage was about 50 per cent or 60 per cent and not the 90 per cent threshold that warrants an angioplasty. And in some of the cases, the angiography showed that there was no blockage at all, yet the hospital went ahead with the stenting!

9

Too Much of a Good Thing

Healthcare in India can be world class if you have pockets deep enough. You can get top-notch care full of comfort matching that of a luxury hotel. However, at the other end of the spectrum are government hospitals with their filthy corridors, defunct equipment and rude doctors who are stressed by the teeming crowds vying for their attention while being shoved around by guards. Government initiatives to calm inflationary trends in healthcare are aimed at the less affluent. The eligibility criteria for government insurance schemes are strict and sometimes people are excluded on grounds such as owning a motorcycle or a refrigerator. That puts them in the 'missing middle' category, the people not 'poor enough' to be eligible for government programmes but unable to afford private insurance. Norms tend to disregard the fact that we live in an era of EMIs, when owning consumer durables is easier than ever before, provided one is willing to pay a nominal interest.

People in this category choose the private sector not for a luxurious experience but because it is more accessible, free of the delays that plague government hospitals. For instance, the waiting period for orthopaedic surgeries at AIIMS in New Delhi is now about a year.[1] A patient in need of an MRI scan may need to wait for a period of three years.[2] For these patients, private hospitals can sometimes be a lifesaver. They should not face bankruptcy for accessing timely care. Yet regulation of the private sector is a long pending healthcare reform.

There is another aspect of how healthcare is dispensed in the private sector that has immediate implications for the overall public health of the country. It pertains to irrational drug use.

India's lax regulatory architecture has for years glossed over the menace of over-the-counter sale of prescription medicines. The vast army of quacks and crosspathy practitioners (doctors who are trained in one system of medicine but prescribe drugs from a different system with scant regard for prescription norms) add to the complicated mix. This is now impacting efforts to eliminate endemic infectious diseases such as tuberculosis, with India having among the highest numbers in the world of drug-resistant forms of the bacterial infection.[3] That is why prescription audit is becoming an area of heightened academic interest.

The ICMR recently funded a study that looked at the prescription practices of doctors at both government and private hospitals. The findings were published in the ICMR's in-house publication *Indian Journal of Medical Research* and revealed appalling levels of violations with 45 per cent of the assessed prescriptions being deviant.[4] One in ten prescriptions was found to have 'unacceptable' deviations from the norm. The most frequently prescribed drugs were pantoprazole (a proton pump inhibitor prescribed for acid reflux), a combination drug of rabeprazole and domperidone (used to treat ulcers in the intestine and to fight nausea) and oral enzyme preparations (for indigestion).

Upper respiratory tract infection (URTI) and hypertension were the most common diseases for which prescriptions had unacceptable deviations. Cost implications were the most common consequence of the deviations with 63 per cent of the aberrant prescriptions leading to a rise in the cost of treatment. But that was not the only undesirable side effect of bad prescriptions. They also led to patients becoming more susceptible to adverse drug reactions, which could necessitate more healthcare spending in the long term. However, the study did not delve into that aspect.

In some cases, antacids and proton pump inhibitors were pre-emptively prescribed to counter possible side effects of analgesics prescribed in a patient who came with, say, a complaint of knee pain. However, long-term use of proton pump inhibitors is associated with multiple side effects, one of which is a higher risk of fractures in older people. Brittle bones can lead to aches and pains – it is possible for patients to get stuck in a vicious loop of a drug being given for the primary complaint and having to take another to deal with the side effects of the first drug only to find that the second drug triggers its own set of side effects, some of which include the primary complaint! Violation of prescription norms can have devastating consequences. Imagine the implications for a 60-year-old osteoporotic woman who goes to the doctor with knee pain but the medication she is given, while reducing her pain, makes it more likely for her to end up with a fractured limb!

The researchers who conducted the study are from some of the top institutes in the country, including AIIMS and Christian Medical College, Vellore. They accept that the prescriptions with unacceptable deviations could have been prescribed by junior doctors who have to cater to a large number of patients and are not able to prioritise and multitask. 'Besides this, inadequate emphasis on rational prescribing in medical curriculum and drug promotion by pharmaceutical industries may also have contributed to the inappropriate prescribing and non-compliance to guidelines,' write the researchers in the paper. However, they did not compare the prescribing practices of senior and junior doctors but pointed out that when irrational prescriptions are handed out, it is the patient who suffers. To resolve this problem, the researchers suggested that rational prescribing habits be inculcated amongst medical students right from their undergraduate days. These principles then need to be reinforced during their professional development.

Unfortunately, ICMR has no legal mandate to regulate the medical profession. The union health ministry has the mandate to bring in, if they so wish, statutory backing for regular prescription audits. It prefers to lay accountability at the doors of individual state governments.

However, doctors defend their prescription practices by arguing that they cater to what their assessment is of a patient's expectations. 'If a patient consults with me and I do not write them a prescription, they will go away thinking that I am not a competent doctor and will never return,' says a physician working as a consultant for a hospital chain. 'A prescription makes people feel like they have derived value for the fee they paid. If I do not do so, they will go to another doctor who will write those medicines anyway. So I lose a patient, and the reason why I risk losing them is not served either. So even if nothing is needed, I will probably prescribe some supplements to at least ensure there is some placebo effect.'

Placebo effect is a phenomenon in which a person uses a substance, with no therapeutic value, with the belief that it will make them better and then reports an improvement in symptoms. However, not all patients yearn for prescriptions, especially for supplements that can cost over ₹50 per pill. Gayatri Mathew recounts the time her mother was admitted to a hospital after a brief spell of dengue that sent her platelets plummeting. Her platelet count was around 65,000 when hospitalisation was advised. Gayatri later found out that it was usually not until the reading fell to the 30,000–40,000 range that a patient was hospitalised, so her mother could have still been managed at home. But she presumed that the doctor may have been taking extra precautions keeping her age in mind. But at the time of discharge, her medical summary included a prescription for a host of supplements, some of which were prohibitively expensive. 'My regular doctor took a look at them and asked me to send them back to the pharmacy,' she says.

The corridors of corporate hospitals are regularly stalked by medical representatives, who are easily recognised by their formal clothes and leather briefcases, usually full of pamphlets for a range of medicines and supplements. Their job is to convince doctors that their products are superior to the competitors' and should be used in patients for best results. Both scientific evidence and financial inducements are used. Doctors, in their turn use both clinical judgement and their assessment of the patient's spending power to prescribe supplements that may or may not be essential.

Many of these drugs are manufactured by small and relatively unknown pharmaceutical companies. Many doctors who have encountered these sales pitches have also chosen not to succumb to them. The transactions between these medical representatives and doctors have been mentioned in several books authored by doctors and have even been discussed in courts during legal proceedings. The acknowledgement of this nexus has fuelled many attempts at regulations that delegitimise these 'deals'.

A COVID-19 star

In 2022, a company called Apex Laboratories had approached the Supreme Court of India with an unusual request.[5]

It appealed against a decision of the Income Tax Appellate Tribunal to uphold the decision of an income tax commissioner to treat as income the 'expenditure' of ₹4,72,91,159 incurred by the company towards gifts such as gold coins, TVs, fridges and laptops for medical practitioners for 'creating awareness' about the health supplement 'Zincovit'. It was unusual because existing regulations did not allow medical practitioners to accept these gifts. The tribunal's decision made the sum taxable.

The petition was dismissed, with the court observing that medical practitioners have a 'quasi-fiduciary relationship' with their patients. A doctor's prescription is considered to be the final word on the treatment, even if the cost of the medication is barely within the financial means of the patient. Such is the level of trust reposed in doctors. 'Therefore, it is a matter of great public importance and concern when it is demonstrated that a doctor's prescription can be manipulated,' warned the court, which also noted that the cost of supplying freebies including sponsorships for foreign trips or medical conferences is factored into the price of the drug, thus creating a 'perpetual publicly injurious cycle'. The danger of doctors prescribing medication that is significantly marked up over effective generic counterparts, for reasons that are not clinical, had also perturbed the Parliamentary Standing Committee on Health and Family Welfare.'[6] The committee had noted that the patently illegal practice of giving gifts to doctors from pharmaceutical companies has an inflationary effect on medicine prices as the cost of gifts such as air conditioners, cars, music systems and gold chains get added to the cost of drugs.

Zincovit, a drug containing zinc and various other vitamins, became a familiar name during the COVID-19 pandemic at a time when there were no vaccines yet and medical science was still uncertain what medicines would work against the SARS-CoV-2 virus. It seemed then that the only thing that prevented the virus from being fatal was one's own immunity. The idea of zinc as an immunity booster caught on and soon zinc supplements became all the rage. By October 2020, Zincovit had become the leader in the domestic pharmaceutical market.[7] This was the first time ever that a multivitamin had managed to take the top spot, ahead of medicines for lifestyle ailments such as diabetes.

A question may be asked retrospectively, in the light of subsequent revelations, about how much of that success was thanks to its manufacturer's generosity in handing out freebies. But the question of repercussions of supplement overuse came to haunt the country soon enough. In the wake of the deadly second wave of COVID in 2021, caused by the delta variant of the SARS-CoV-2, came the mucormycosis outbreak. The fungal infection started prolonging hospitalisation and adding to the number of fatalities. Doctors quickly realised that the indiscriminate use of zinc may have had a role to play in the proliferation of the lethal black fungus.

Researchers at the Post Graduate Institute of Medical Education and Research (PGIMER), Chandigarh, tried to grow black fungus in the laboratory and found that when the medium used is enriched with zinc, some of the fungus isolates thrived. However, they cautioned that their study does not conclusively support the hypothesis that zinc supplementation contributed to the pathogenesis of mucormycosis, and more data was needed to confirm the hypothesis. Whether India's mucormycosis outbreak would have been less severe had there not been a population-level overuse of zinc during the early days of the pandemic is a question for scientists and policymakers to mull over. But the correlations do demonstrate how far-reaching the consequences of supplement overuse can be.

Despite the Supreme Court judgement and observation in the Apex Laboratories case, little was done to change the structural loopholes in the regulatory framework. That was once again evident in September 2024, when the central government notified the Uniform Code for Marketing Practices in Medical Devices (UCMPMD), which outlawed foreign trips and monetary incentives for medical professionals.[8] The marketing strategies of the drug and medical devices industry are often very similar, with one taking cues from the other. Only the financials are vastly different; medical equipment is significantly more expensive so the 'marketing expenses' for one such high-end machine can be the same as that spent on several drugs to achieve high volumes of sales. India's poor domestic manufacturing volumes add a premium even to the most basic equipment. Conscious of the price sensitivity of the market, companies selling medical devices sometimes offer the machines at a nominal cost, profiting instead from the reagents or consumables that are used. When it comes to contentious marketing strategies deployed by the pharmaceutical industry, it does not always have to be gifts to individual doctors. They can also be lavish medical conferences and CME sessions. That is why the UCMPMD lays down well-defined, transparent and verifiable set of procedures for the engagement of the medical device industry with healthcare professionals at CMEs or at conferences, seminars and workshops. It also expressly forbids foreign CMEs without prior permission from the government's department of pharmaceuticals. The industry is undaunted.

Towards the end of 2024, the department of pharmaceuticals pulled up a company called Abbvie Healthcare for splurging over ₹1 crore on sponsoring a trip for 30 doctors to Monaco and Paris. The stated purpose of the trip was to offer knowledge about Botox and Juvederm.[9] The NMC has now started a probe in the matter. Dodgy pharmaceutical marketing practices are used as much for private practitioners as for doctors attached to corporate hospitals, but the cost implications of overprescription are amplified in corporate hospitals. The ICMR study did not look at that aspect.

Manipulation of medical decision-making can happen at many levels, all with some degree of complicity of medical practitioners. Pharmaceutical companies have now started to influence peer-reviewed medical journals, which are seen as the cornerstone of medical practice. These publications help doctors stay abreast of the latest medical developments, standardise treatment protocols based on outcomes in other hospitals and other countries and reassess risks based on various case reports. In many institutions, particularly those that are publicly funded, the career progression of doctors is linked to the number of papers published in peer-reviewed journals.

A senior consultant, who was once part of an AIIMS-like institution and is now also associated with a medical journal, says that pharmaceutical companies have started approaching amenable doctors with offers of financial compensation in return for lending their names to papers in peer-reviewed medical journals. The doctor who is thus courted, may not have worked on that paper at all, yet they would become the lead author and lend credibility to it. The paper would promote one of the company's products. It is a win-win for both parties. The advantage for the company is getting the endorsement of a doctor that will help boost their sales. And the doctor gets one more paper in their name without having done any work on it.

'We often get papers that have serious red flags,' says the consultant. 'As peers we know the lead author of the paper has not participated in the clinical trial but has just agreed to lend his name for other considerations. We reject those. However, many other journals – knowingly or otherwise – publish them.' The retraction rate – which measures the percentage of published scientific papers that are withdrawn after publication – has been going up in recent years, even for top global journals.

A top pharmacologist at a government hospital says that there is a need to analyse and study prescription practices in the private sector to truly understand the trends and factors leading to drug overuse. But consent – both from patients and doctors – is difficult to secure. 'We had planned such a study but it got into a legal tangle over concerns about data privacy. The Ayushman Bharat Digital Mission (ABDM) may make [conducting] such analysis easier in the future, but the concern about consent would still need to be addressed,' they said.

ABDM is a plan to use India's digital prowess to build a health infrastructure that can make healthcare efficient, accessible, inclusive and affordable. One of the pillars of that plan is archiving and storing personal health records of individuals, each of whom will be assigned a unique health ID in the form of a 14-digit number. All the records will be available at the click of a mouse and each person would exclusively control access to their records to prevent their misuse.

Antimicrobial resistance

Recent conversations in India about issues such as prescription hygiene and regulation of over-the-counter sale of drugs were triggered by the worldwide clamour about antimicrobial resistance in pathogens. When pathogens are exposed to antibiotics at a suboptimal dose or for a duration insufficient for their elimination, they tend to metamorphose into versions of themselves that are no longer vulnerable to that antibiotic class. India was unfairly associated with antibiotic resistance when an enzyme that confers resistance to pathogens against some of the most used antibiotics was named after the Indian capital.

The New Delhi Metallo Beta-Lactamase-1 (NDM-1) was first identified in December 2009 in a Swedish national who, researchers thought, had contracted the infection in India. The Indian government was not happy with the name and *The Lancet* later acknowledged that the enzyme had been wrongly named as pathogens harbouring that protein had been identified in many other cities in other parts of the world.[10] But the controversy had an unintended fallout; it forced our government to acknowledge and at least notionally attempt to address the regulatory loopholes that made India a fertile breeding ground for drug-resistant, disease-producing organisms.

Now India has a National Action Plan for antimicrobial resistance and several regulations have been implemented to ensure antibiotics are not sold without prescriptions over the counter. Many corporate hospitals also have antibiotic stewards to ensure there is no overuse of antibiotics. Recent analyses have shown that there are still many problems with how antibiotics are prescribed, used and sold in India. However, antibiotics did not feature among the top three most inappropriately prescribed drugs in the IJMR study. Azithromycin, an antibiotic commonly prescribed for ailments such as throat infections, came fifth in the list, with the only other antibiotic in the top ten being cefixime, which is used to treat bacterial infections.

Dr Neelima Kshirsagar, the national chair for clinical pharmacology at ICMR and one of the authors of the study, says, 'There are two things one needs to remember when looking at that study – first, we were looking at only OPD prescriptions. In our assessment, there are comparatively a lot more antibiotics prescribed for inpatients than outpatients. The second thing is that we looked at a few thousand (4,838) prescriptions in a country of 1.4 billion. The results show only a small part of the actual problem,' she claims. 'Not all prescriptions had the diagnosis mentioned, and we could assess the rationality of the prescription only where it was mentioned.'

Broad-spectrum antibiotics are widely used in corporate hospitals. In 2022, a study published in *The Lancet Regional Health Southeast Asia* flagged that problem when it concluded: 'Although the per-capita private-sector consumption rate of antibiotics in India is relatively low compared to many countries, India consumes a large volume of broad-spectrum antibiotics that should ideally be used sparingly. This, together with significant share of fixed-dose combinations (FDCs) from formulations outside NLEM and a large volume of antibiotics not approved by the central drug regulators, call for significant policy and regulatory reform.'[11]

FDCs or fixed dose combinations add to India's longstanding regulatory issues. Pharmaceutical companies often combine two drugs into a single one with fixed proportions of each drug. There are many problems with this practice, linked to a mismatch of the rates at which the drugs are metabolised, reactions between the two because of common metabolic pathways and concerns about shelf life. Every few years the drug regulator bans certain FDC drugs. But new ones keep entering the market and quickly gain favour with medical practitioners until being outlawed by a fresh regulation. As a rule, an FDC of two or more drugs will cost more than what each of those drugs individually cost. The side effects are also often unknown.

Lack of antibiotic prescription hygiene is an endemic problem in the country. A neurosurgeon at a premier government hospital in Delhi reveals that they get many referrals from private hospitals when the recovery period is long and the patient has run out of money or exhausted their insurance cover. 'In such patients we routinely see third-generation cephalosporins (a class of advanced antibiotics) being used where first-generation cephalosporins should have been the drug of choice. Advanced antibiotics such as carbapenems and vancomycin are used for minor illnesses,' he says.

'It is very important for institutes to have defined protocols for antibiotic use that are sacrosanct.' He adds that in his own hospital there is a strict system of categorising patients as 'clean', 'clean contaminated', 'contaminated' and 'dirty' based on the levels of drug resistance they might have. 'Antibiotics are administered accordingly,' he explains. 'Regardless of seniority, everybody must abide by this protocol.' The hospital where this neurosurgeon works is considered one of the best government hospitals in the country and is known to practise medicine ethically and systematically. Its clinical results are at par with the best hospitals in developed countries.

But not all government facilities tick these boxes. When it comes to antibiotic overuse, government hospitals and health centres are as culpable as private establishments. In 2021–2022, the National Centre for Disease Control (NCDC) – the government organisation mandated with the tracking and epidemiological analysis of diseases – commissioned a study on antibiotic use at 20 hospitals in the National Antibiotic Consumption Network (NAC-NET). A survey was conducted across the length and breadth of the country over a six-month period.[12] It found that in 55 per cent of cases, antibiotics had been prescribed as a preventive measure. This was flagged in the report as one of the reasons for taking action to prevent non-judicious use of antibiotics. The report also called for prescription audits at individual hospitals to encourage appropriate antibiotic use.

India is paying a very high price for its cavalier attitude towards regulating prescription and sale of antibiotics. The Washington-based Institute of Health Metrics and Evaluation, which conducts the Global Burden of Disease Study, estimates that in 2019 there were 2,97,000 deaths attributable to anti-microbial resistance (AMR) – commonly referred to as drug resistance – in India. AMR, it said, kills more people in India than cancer and tuberculosis.[13] However, the perception about corporate hospitals as the biggest practitioners of unethical medicine is fallacious when it comes to antibiotic overuse. In reality, these are entities that have to abide by medical and regulatory compliance norms, go through accreditation checks and employ qualified doctors. Several national and international accreditation boards give their stamp of approval to many of these hospitals after stringent, periodic inspections.

In India's vast hinterlands, where quacks abound and almost anybody can establish a hospital, prescription regulations are not only unheard of but also virtually impossible to implement. Medical care is dispensed mostly by untrained practitioners, a fact acknowledged even by the government when it roped in these 'informal' healthcare providers for the Revised National Tuberculosis Control Programme (RNTCP). Researchers from Canada, Australia and India published a paper in the *BMJ Global Health* on 'Unlocking the Potential of Informal Healthcare Providers in Tuberculosis Care', which highlights the importance of this approach. The researchers talked about the widespread presence of these informal practitioners and the strong acceptance that they have within their communities, where they frequently serve as the first port of call for patients seeking healthcare.

The prevalence of untrained medicinal practitioners in India's health system landscape is also evident from WHO's India Health Workforce report. This report indicates that a significant portion of those identified as allopathic doctors lack formal medical training. In fact, 57.3 per cent do not have any medical qualifications while a remarkable 31.4 per cent of these individuals have only a secondary school education.[14] These informal 'doctors' are also the first step on the slippery slope of drug resistance, prescribing weak doses of antibiotics which lead to eventual resistance in the pathogen.

India is already teetering on the edge of an AMR crisis, with multiple warnings over the last couple of decades having gone largely unheeded. Prescription audits, stricter checks on drug sales and mandatory refresher courses for individual practitioners would be the first steps in the effort to stalling and eventually reversing this menace.

10

Medicine Beyond Borders

The Transplantation of Human Organs and Tissues Act, 1994 mandates that if an organ is removed from a person's body while they are alive, then it can only be transplanted in a close relative. The only exception to that is when a close relative is willing to donate but is not biologically compatible, and there is another donor who is compatible and has a relative in need of an organ. In such cases an organ swap can happen: X donates to A, who is a relative of B, while B donates to Y, who is a relative of X. Many such swaps have happened in different parts of the country.

However, accepting or offering money or other inducements for the donation of any human tissue or organ is a punishable offence. Hospitals have an obligation to ensure that any transplant that happens is not in breach of the law; else they risk being held criminally liable. Dr Hasim Anwer was nearing the end of his shift when he was suddenly told that he was to urgently join a meeting being held in the transplant department of the corporate hospital where he worked.

He was to assist with interpreting for a patient from a neighbouring country and his prospective kidney donor. No member of the transplant authorisation committee of the hospital could understand the only language both men could communicate in, but Dr Anwer could. When he reached the meeting room, he found that it was an on-camera proceeding where the committee (with in-house representatives alongside members from the Delhi government) was trying to reach a decision about the legality of the offer to donate. The question they were grappling with was whether the donor was really related to the foreign patient. The documentation seemed foolproof but what was foremost in the minds of every committee member was a question about their veracity. Instances of forged documents being submitted are not uncommon, and there was no way for them to track whether the donor received financial compensation back in their home country.

It was immediately obvious to Dr Anwer that the potential donor and the patient belonged to very different socioeconomic groups. The patient appeared to be wealthy, while the donor seemed to be a poor man, perhaps a daily wager. Dr Anwer asked him how he was related to the patient. He replied that he was his 'chacha' (uncle). 'I asked him where he lived, and he named a small town in their home country. But when I asked where his uncle lived, he could not give a clear reply. How does a man who is donating an organ to his "uncle" out of love for him not know where that uncle lives?' says Dr Anwer incredulously. 'I knew there was something wrong. A few more random questions were enough to convince me that this was a case of a rich man buying an organ from a poor man.'

Dr Anwer says that the committee could not have missed the fumbling and shifty replies to their questions. 'However, at that point, a senior administrator interrupted the conversation and asked a staff member to bring me something to eat,' he recalls. 'As the committee began looking at the papers the men had submitted, I realised that the documentation was perfectly in order. My job had been to just translate, not draw conclusions from what I was hearing. Nobody asked my opinion. The transplant was cleared.'

India's medical tourism industry, helmed largely by the private sector is valued at $10 million and expected to steadily rise in the coming years. Most foreign patients are from the Southeast Asia region – Afghanistan, Bangladesh (temporarily staggered following the regime change in that country and a chill in relations with India, though medical visas continue to be issued by India), Pakistan (stopped a few years ago), Myanmar, Cambodia – and from several African nations and the former CIS countries. Patients also fly in from developed countries such as the UK and the USA, as medical and surgical expenses are significantly less here; some are forced to look for other options because of a long waiting period such as in the National Health Service in the UK.

An analysis[1] in 2020 found that a heart bypass surgery that costs \$144,000 in the United States could be done in India for as low as \$3,000. An American medical tourist would pay anything between \$3,000 and \$6,500 for an angioplasty that would cost \$57,000 in their home country. Knee replacement procedures billed in the US at \$50,000 could cost \$3,500 to \$8,500 in India. Even a relatively simple procedure such as a dental implant could cost less than half of the American rate of \$2,800 in India. To woo foreign patients, many Indian hospitals choose to get certified by international organisations such as Joint Commission International and Global Healthcare Accreditation – organisations that they are more familiar with than Indian accreditation bodies. Medical tourism is a matter of great pride for India and a source of valuable foreign exchange, which is why the government launched the 'Heal in India' programme to encourage the inflow of foreign patients by easing visa requirements and other procedural formalities.

Late Amit Sengupta, a public health activist, believed that some of the additional income from foreign patients should be used to treat Indian patients who cannot afford quality healthcare. In 2008, he wrote an article in the *Indian Journal of Medical Ethics* in which he pointed out that the government gives private hospitals treating foreign patients benefits such as lower import duties and an increased rate of depreciation for life-saving medical equipment.[2] Foreign patients are treated like royalty and given special meals as part of their package. A translator who has a proven track record in bringing business from abroad to the hospital where they work can command a salary to rival that of senior doctors.

But competition is fierce. There are many private hospitals vying for a share of the medical tourism pie. Patients applying for an Indian medical visa need to submit a letter issued by the hospital where they intend to get their treatment. This means that foreign patients must know which hospital in India they are headed to before they leave their home countries. The challenge for Indian hospitals therefore is to reach prospective foreign patients in their home countries and convince them.

Hospitals quickly realised the importance of local outreach in foreign countries. Most corporate hospitals that receive a significant number of foreign patients now have tie-ups with medical establishments in the countries from which most of these patients come. These overseas partners facilitate visits by senior doctors from Indian hospitals, allow them to use their facilities to see patients and refer them to their parent hospitals for surgeries. Once these patients return home, the local partners also help with follow-ups. Most Indian doctors are licensed to practice only within their own country unless they hold an international registration, such as with the General Medical Council in the United Kingdom. It is the prerogative of the host countries to allow these doctors to practise there, and they often do so, because the foreign doctors compensate for their own shortage of qualified medical personnel.

Occasionally, overeager hospitals or doctors will try to game the system and pay for it. In 2022, the Bangladesh Medical and Dental Council disallowed two Indian doctors for issuing advertisements targeting Bangladeshi patients without first registering with the council.[3] A senior doctor at a corporate hospital chain says he has made several such trips to various countries and found that the process of registration and obtaining local permissions varies from country to country, but nowhere is it easy.

Corporate hospitals usually get their doctors the permission to see patients with the help of their local partners. For some countries, obtaining the permission to visit may need some off-the-record payments. A local partner can help with that too. Video conferencing options are used to reach out to patients, but in-person interactions are best to build equity and trust. 'That is why we need to travel,' concludes the senior doctor.

Patients are referred to Indian hospitals for interventions that are either not available or not affordable in their home country.

The model works better for disciplines where the average cost of treatment is higher, so surgical disciplines are often the ones reaching out the most to foreign patients. According to figures given out by the National Organ and Tissue Transplant (NOTTO) in 2023, of the 18,336 organ recipients in India that year, 1,851 were foreign nationals.[4] An organ transplant from a living donor can cost anything between ₹20 lakh and ₹40 lakh, depending on the facility and the organ transplanted. They are easily among the most expensive surgical procedures carried out in Indian hospitals.

It is common for organ transplant surgeons to travel to foreign destinations in search of patients. One such doctor reveals the 'simple arrangement' in which he visits a country for a couple of days and sees patients brought in by the local partner of the hospital he works for. 'For those that need transplants, I give them the option of getting the procedure done in India,' he says. 'If they have the resources to travel, our hospital issues the invitation letter, and they get their visas within a few weeks.'

The prices that international patients pay for surgeries in India are typically 20 per cent to 30 per cent higher than what is charged from Indian patients. 'Things like manpower, drugs, consumables and bed remain the same for foreign patients, but there are minor upgrades in the quality of food and floor managers are told to be extra attentive to these patients,' reveals another doctor who treats international patients frequently. 'Through the markup in price for the same service, the hospital recovers all the extra costs of operating an overseas partnership and sending consultants abroad.'

The families of foreign patients also have to pay for a fairly prolonged stay in India because a lot of time is required for post-surgery follow-ups. A transplant recipient must take immunosuppressive drugs for life to ensure that their body does not reject the foreign body that has been introduced in the form of the transplanted organ. These drugs blunt the natural responses of the immune system, which makes transplant patients more susceptible to infections, particularly opportunistic ones like tuberculosis.

The drugs are given in higher doses immediately after the surgery and then tapered down over time. It is a while before the patient is ready to take the flight back home, and in the meantime their family can easily spend over ₹40,000 per month just on their living expenses in India. In fact, small feeder economies revolving around services to foreign patients and their families thrive around many tertiary care hospitals in various cities.

A dark underbelly

But the dark side of the transplant industry hides under the glitter of big numbers, the laudatory media coverage highlighting the quality of Indian healthcare and the boost that it gives to the national economy. Sordid tales of transgressions and commissions surface only occasionally before being quickly tucked away into the recesses of the system as business and political interests take precedence. In his impromptu role as a translator for a foreign patient, Dr Anwer could get a sneak peek into that darkness. However, there are many other more detailed accounts that are publicly available.

In December 2023, UK-based *The Telegraph* published a report on the findings of its undercover reporter in Myanmar.[5] Posing as a distraught relative looking for an organ donor, the reporter approached an agent and was offered a transplant package at a prominent Delhi hospital. He was given a full estimate on the hospital's letterhead. The agent then told the reporter about the people who had 'bought' organs from their fellow countrymen and the documents that were then doctored for the purposes of compliance to Indian transplant laws.

The agent assured the undercover reporter that he would, for the right price, 'make arrangements' to ensure that the donor and the recipient could pass as family members. This included property registration documents that showed that both lived in the same house, 'old' family photos, fictional family trees. The reporter was also introduced to a person who had allegedly received an organ from a person he did not know and had undergone the procedure in India.

After the report was published, the hospital named in it admitted that the person the reporter had spoken to was its representative in the country but denied any knowledge of wrongdoings. However, this was disputed by the locals in Myanmar, who insisted that the hospital wilfully chose to look the other way. The newspaper also published photos of the hospital's star kidney transplant surgeon, attending an organ transplant event at a glitzy hotel in Myanmar. Both the doctor and this hospital had also found themselves mired in allegations of complicity in an organ transplant racket back in 2016, when they were accused of transplanting kidneys that had been illegally acquired from poor people in West Bengal.[6] The alleged donors were paid a pittance. The hospital issued a statement at the time claiming that those accused of being involved in the alleged racket were not employees of the hospital but secretarial staff working with some of their doctors. The hospital claimed to have been a victim of a well-orchestrated operation to cheat patients with fake and forged documents.

A few months later, the *The Indian Express* published a report on organ transplant rackets thriving in Delhi hospitals using fake family trees and cooked up diagnostic reports. These alleged racketeers even bypassed diplomatic scrutiny, the report claimed.[7] In July 2024, Delhi Police arrested several people suspected of involvement in a kidney transplant racket, including a doctor who was associated with two hospitals, one in Delhi and one in Noida. Both hospitals quickly dissociated themselves from her. The documents unearthed during the investigation revealed that letters with the doctor's letterhead, in some cases signed by her, were misused by various people to issue the documents required to obtain approval from the hospital's transplant authorisation committee. If the clearance was not obtained at one hospital, the doctor allegedly went to the other and repeated the process to get the approval there.[8]

Even three decades after the law banning organ trade came into force, such rackets continue to thrive. It is an indicator of how pervasive and deep-rooted the problem is. There are many structural reasons why organ transplants remain a potentially murky medical discipline. Hospitals go all out to court foreign patients, often resorting to questionable means to secure these high-paying customers. After concerns were raised in the highest echelons of the government, the ministry of health and family welfare is said to have been considering implementing a system in which these prospective patients are assigned to specific hospitals based on a transparent system by the Indian embassies in their countries rather than letting hospitals compete with each other for their business.[9] The ministry of external affairs has also been asked to appoint a nodal officer for coordinating organ transplants for foreign patients.[10]

India is perpetually underserved when it comes to organs available for transplant. According to an estimate published in 2023 in the *International Journal of General Medicine*, of the 2,58,000 organs (1,85,000 kidneys, 33,000 livers and 50,000 hearts) needed every year in India, only 6,000 kidneys, 1,200 livers and 15 hearts are transplanted annually. The only way to bridge this gap is to encourage cadaver organ donations. Families have to be counselled to donate the organs of brain-dead patients and individuals killed in traffic accidents, but religious beliefs and personal qualms have thwarted progress on that front.

Chronic organ shortage in a poverty-stricken country make for a deadly cocktail. Madhubabu Garlapati, 31, an autorickshaw driver in Guntur, learned this the hard way when he responded to a Facebook post promising ₹30 lakh for a kidney. Madhubabu claims that he had agreed to the plea in the hope of using the money to repay a loan and to give his children a better life. But after his organ was allegedly removed at a super-specialty hospital in Vijayawada, he was paid only ₹50,000.[11] After complaining to the Guntur police, he told the media that he found that fake documents had been created with a changed address to show him as a relative of the recipient. The hospital, however, claims that the due process of law was followed and that it has documents to prove it.

This is not an isolated case. On social media, there are many groups run for people seeking organs. Posts asking for various organs from people of specific blood groups, with some even stating the amount they would pay are common in these fora. One such post that I found states: 'Need donors with Indian passport, age 25 to 35, amount 5.5 lakh. Inbox me.' Another says: 'Need O+ kidney donor from Tamil Nadu. Family permission compulsory. Age below 40. Very urgent. Message me.' In December 2023, NOTTO had to send out a circular to all state governments reminding them that social media posts offering or asking for organs in exchange for compensation are also in violation of the law. However, there are still thriving closed groups on social media where users seek and participate in organ trade.[12]

A prominent Mumbai-based transplant surgeon declares that organ trade flourishes because hospitals choose profits over ethics. 'Even when all documents are in order, there are red flags in some cases,' he reveals. 'Hospitals can choose whether to act on them or not.' One of the 'red flags' he mentions is a marked disparity in the socioeconomic status of the donor and the recipient. He says sarcastically: 'I always say that the drivers of Mumbai's rich and famous are the most loving. They always donate out of the "goodness" of their hearts.'

Many transplant surgeons now say that the experience of the last few decades makes a strong case for accepting that the very concept of altruistic donations – the basis of India's organ transplant law – is detached from reality. They say it may be a more rational approach to try to ringfence the donor as much as possible, if not with overt payments, then at least with government incentives such as health insurance. Alternatively organ donation could be used as a criterion for eligibility for other government programmes. Their contention is that it may be better to accept the reality that most organ donors receive compensation under the table anyway. Rather than turning a blind eye to this, allowing for legal forms of compensation could also ensure that the donor, who may have lifelong health issues, is also adequately cared for.

However, there is a deeper murkiness in the transplant industry that goes beyond just the malpractices of corporate hospitals. A transplant surgeon who practises in Delhi-NCR says that it is simplistic to put the onus of all wrongdoings on corporate hospitals. He reveals that in some states, clerks in government offices will seek a small cash gratification just for the convening of the transplant authorisation committee. 'Hospitals do not have any option but to pay up because otherwise sick patients will end up waiting far longer for a transplant than is necessary,' he complains.

Some hospitals make the minutes of their transplant authorisation committee meetings publicly available. Scrutiny of some of these records reveals that approvals are routine and rejections rare. The surgeon explains that this is because transplant coordinators at most top hospitals are very careful about the files they put before the committee. 'I recently had a patient from Bangladesh here for a liver transplant, with his wife as the donor,' he says. 'After several of us hospital officials spoke to them, there was no doubt in our minds that they were indeed husband and wife. But the problem was that they were not very educated and did not have any documents to present as evidence. The transplant coordinators said the case was sure to be rejected by the committee so we did not present it.' By the time the couple's children arrived from Bangladesh with the required documentation, the patient had passed away.

Beyond transplants

There are also many instances of patients who come to India to be treated at a specific hospital without any outreach on the part of the hospital. These are more affluent patients from countries where medicine is not as well developed, including some African nations and some of our Asian neighbours. These patients have multiple-entry medical visas and are familiar with India. A senior doctor at a corporate hospital mentions a recent patient from an African nation who had developed weakness in his limbs. He had been treated with steroids in his home country but did not feel any improvement in his condition, so he just flew to Delhi. 'We did a few tests, found that he was suffering from Guillain-Barre Syndrome (GBS). In his own country they had not even managed to diagnose his ailment correctly. This is the equity India has built internationally as a competent and world-class medical system. People trust us and we are good.'

Other top specialties that attract foreign patients to India are cardiac surgery, orthopaedics, plastic surgery, oncology and trauma care. An additional draw in recent years has been India's traditional medicine. An increasing number of yoga retreats offer special packages for foreign patients. For patients from the USA or Europe, who are covered by insurance, hospitals issue an official estimate that the patient gets approved by their insurance provider. Then, the patient can avail cashless treatment in India while the payment is transferred to the hospital's account from the foreign insurance company. However, most foreign patients are without insurance cover, which means they are charged rates that are higher than what their counterparts with insurance are quoted.

A senior doctor explains that while foreign patients are good for business, they are also labelled 'handle with care' – an administrative terminology used by hospitals for patients who are well connected. Any dispute or controversy involving foreign patients can quickly escalate into a diplomatic matter with the foreign embassy getting involved. 'If there is an untoward incident such as a death while in our care, there will be investigations that may snowball into something bigger,' he explains. 'That is why we are all extra careful if the patient is a foreign national.' Despite this caution, cases of medical negligence and corporate bullying still surface and occasionally foreign patients are forced to knock the doors of Indian courts.

In 2022, Yemen resident Mahfood Qasem Ali Al Garadi approached the Delhi High Court asking for the court's intervention to retrieve the passports of his wife and infant son from a super-specialty hospital that had confiscated them after a dispute over the bill for the treatment of his son. The young boy was suffering from a spinal cord ailment. Their petition also alleged that the hospital and an interpreter had swindled the couple, who claimed that they were being forced to pay double the amount ($7,000 to $7,500) that had been initially given as the estimate for treatment.

The court ordered the passports to be returned and told the couple that they could seek compensation from the hospital. The embassy of Yemen intervened, leading to the swift firing of all officials in the International Patient Services department at the hospital who were involved with this patient in these transactions. The hospital issued a statement that this was a one-off instance of malpractice and not something that foreign patients routinely encounter at their establishment.

A corporate hospital doctor who sees a lot of foreign patients reveals that patients from advanced nations ask more questions, are better informed and usually speak English. Many of them have insurance policies that ensure there is a certain level of scrutiny of the bill. 'But patients from countries where English is not commonly spoken and insurance penetration is poor – take Afghanistan, for example – are vulnerable to exploitation. Patients from Yemen, Kazakhstan and Turkmenistan hardly speak English and rarely have insurance,' he says. 'They tend to be overly dependent on their translators, who can collude with doctors to push them into a cycle of unnecessary tests, interventions and medications. It is only when they run out of money or the treatment outcome is not as promised that the matter escalates.'

Deprived even of the rudimentary safeguard that a health insurance offers, they end up paying a lot more than they should. However, he points out that embassies are usually vigilant about malpractice. 'Recently a child from Oman died at my hospital,' he shares. 'The embassy of Oman immediately sought the details of the case and demanded an explanation.' The National Strategy and Roadmap for Medical and Wellness Tourism concedes that there are no regulations to govern the sector, which leaves it unorganised and unmonitored. 'There is a need for greater support from the government towards regulation, facilitation and marketing to position India as a "Medical Value Travel" destination,' it notes.

Corporate hospital doctors are not just sent to foreign destinations to look for patients, nor do the prospective patients have to be candidates for organ transplants. Many smaller medical centres in rural India lack the facilities for advanced surgeries, making these villages and small towns fertile hunting grounds for corporate hospitals. Many major hospital chains have now started holding health camps in remote locations that are managed and coordinated not by clinical departments but by marketing personnel. In fact, the camps are organised under the guise of corporate social responsibility (CSR) activities, serving the dual purpose of bringing in new business while also burnishing the public image of the hospital.

Orthopaedic camps are very popular, as are those conducted by the departments of cardiology and neurology. Following a referral at the camp, many patients travel to the hospital in the city to have joint replacements, prostate surgeries and angioplasties.[13] As in foreign locales, local contacts are vital for the success of such outreach activities. Doctors operating in the area are the first choice for such collaborations and stand to be suitably compensated for their effort. Legally, a doctor cannot split their fee with another doctor for sending patients their way; but there is no bar on commissions to non-medical people. Sometimes financial transactions happen in the name of a family member.

Doctors who have worked for some time in a premier hospital in a big city and then chosen to return to a practice in their hometown are good touchpoints for their former employers or bosses. They frequently refer patients to their former workplaces. This usually begins as an organic process with the doctor sending patients to a setup that they are familiar with, but soon the more enterprising consultants may reach out for a more formal 'arrangement' in which the doctor sends patients specifically to them rather than to the hospital. The states of Northeast India and the hill states of Himachal and Uttarakhand and the union territory of Jammu and Kashmir send a lot of patients to hospitals in Kolkata, Delhi and Chandigarh. The first reports in the media about the ethnic unrest in Manipur in 2023 (that resulted in the imposition of president's rule in the state) emerged when a member of Parliament from Manipur, who had been attacked by a mob, was admitted to a corporate hospital in the national capital.[14]

Some city doctors build such a solid reputation among patients from a particular state that often patients visiting from that region refuse to see other doctors even if they are from the same hospital. 'There is an element of word of mouth for this reputation, but there are also former colleagues who may send them patients,' reveals a doctor. 'There is often a financial arrangement, but there is never any money trail. The deal, where it exists, is usually a personal one between doctors with the institution not [being] involved.'

So pervasive is the practice that at one point the Maharashtra government had seriously considered passing a law making 'cut' a punishable offence.[15] In 2017, surgeon Dr Sanjay Nagral and gastroenterologist Dr Samiran Nundy, two of India's most prominent voices on medical ethics, jointly wrote an opinion piece calling for an end to the practice.[16]

Calling commissions or kickbacks a 'longstanding and widespread' practice in Indian healthcare, they traced its origins to decades old practice of offering an incentive fee to general practitioners for referring patients to specialists. They also pointed out that even large hospitals pay physicians 'facilitation charges' for referring patients to them. The practices have been undeterred both by media reports and the Medical Council of India decreeing in 2012 that fee splitting is unethical.

11

The Cutting Edge

In 2019, Yale School of Medicine compiled a list of medical devices and technology that have enhanced the practice of medicine over centuries. Included in the list were the compound microscope (1590), thermometer (1714), stethoscope (1816), X-ray (1895), cardiac pacemaker (1950) and an artificial pancreas developed at Yale in 2015.[1] Penicillin, the first antibiotic known to humankind, dates back to 1928. It continues to be in use to this day as a broad spectrum antibiotic to treat several ailments including throat and urinary tract infections and even some infections of the brain that can lead to very rapid deterioration of the patient's condition.

The Yale list and the continued relevance of penicillin are evidence that many of the indispensable tools of modern medicine date back a few centuries or at least a few decades.

This is not to take away from the fact that new and evolving technologies are an important part of modern medicine but just like medicines need to be used rationally, so does technology. That discretion can be hard to exercise given the rapidity with which the bench to bed transition is happening – take for example dendritic cell therapy which won a Nobel Prize only in 2011 and is already in widespread use for cancer immunotherapies. But discretion is key, which is why in public health discussions the buzzword is 'appropriate technology' and not 'latest technology'. That power of informed decision-making belongs to a medical professional. But in corporate healthcare, the process of decision-making is often compromised. Instead of the most appropriate technology, the most expensive one is preferred. An example of this is the increasing use of MRI in patients with head trauma, often in lieu of the less expensive and quicker CT scan that doctors say is the gold standard for such cases. Another example is the use of colour dopplers to check for blockages in blood vessels even when that information may not even be relevant for the patient's treatment. The patient ends up paying extra for things that make no difference to treatment outcomes. There is an unstated corporate war that private hospitals are fighting over technology with even incremental upgrades being recorded on billboards and press releases. The taglines have changed from 'First time in India' to 'First time in Southeast Asia', with little or no context of whether they really make a significant difference in the quality of patient care.

In 2019, an article was published in *BMJ Global Health* by researchers from King's College, London, who had explored the impact of corporatisation of healthcare in Maharashtra in collaboration with a Pune-based organisation called Sathi.[2] They found that the two pillars that large corporate hospitals build their reputation on are inpatient 'hospitality' and their use of advanced technology. These infuse irrationalities in medical care while prolonged hospitalisation and excessive diagnostic tests become normalised. These unnecessary tests are performed to ensure returns on the purchase of costly equipment, which can only be achieved with thousands of tests per month. The article concluded that this situation is compounded by the lack of disease-specific testing and treatment guidelines, growing use of private insurance to pay for healthcare and attitudes that see this insurance as legitimising irrational provisions of care.

Regulations governing the medical profession do not allow individual doctors to advertise their services. For example, an endocrinologist running their own clinic cannot advertise their expertise in managing type 2 diabetes, nor can a fertility expert openly flaunt their success rate for invitro fertilisation (IVF). However, corporate hospitals are not bound by these regulations and regularly issue advertisements about their new high value 'acquisitions' – both doctors and new medical equipment. IVF specialist and self-styled activist Dr Aniruddha Malpani calls it the need to 'build a 32-storey building just because my neighbour built 16 storeys, regardless of whether the infrastructure can support that construction. This is because corporate hospitals are competing for patients… A city like Mumbai has about 40 MRI machines. Does it really need so many?' he asks. Each machine can cost about ₹3 crore. He adds that they are acquired by corporate hospitals to steal a march on their rivals, and their patients are overcharged to pay for this unnecessary expense.

In the last couple of decades, medical technology has advanced at a blinding pace worldwide. Over the same period, private healthcare has seen great growth in India. Unfortunately, the country has not been able to establish itself as a manufacturing destination and India has very little skin in the medtech game. It has built capacity to primarily produce high-volume, low-value medical items such as surgical gloves, urinary catheters and other such disposables. In 2023, a joint report by the Public Health Foundation of India and the Indian Medical Parliamentarians' Forum revealed that despite being the world's 20th largest market for medical devices, India houses less than 1.6 per cent of the global industry.[3]

Given the size of the Indian medical device market, global companies are eager to enter it. This motivates them to offer great deals to corporate hospitals for purchase of high-end equipment. One strategy is to offer large commissions on the consumables used in these machines, thereby incentivising their use. A senior public health specialist who has studied the matter for several years explains that even the top 1 per cent of the Indian population with pockets deep enough for insurance coverage, those who can pay for overprescribed and overpriced diagnostic tests, constitutes 'scale' for global medical technology giants. That is why this country of 1.4 billion people is a preferred destination for them.

'In my understanding, private hospitals embrace new technology with the sole motive of making profits. This is one of the main reasons for healthcare inflation in the US, but there the health spend is a fifth of the GDP. In a developing country, more careful consideration needs to go into embracing new technology, unless it's really proven to be scalable. But some of the super-specialty hospitals continue to embrace the American method because they have the clientele,' says the specialist. He adds: 'The triumvirate of insurance, pharmaceuticals and hospital industries have all collectively contributed to this. Another gap when it comes to new technology is that guidelines about their use (mostly international) take some years to come. By that time, they would have already made their money from it.'

In contrast to the excessive haste that private hospitals demonstrate in acquiring new technology, government hospitals have a slow and laborious rate of adoption of these latest machines. This leaves patients who truly need the latest technology to heal with no option but to use private healthcare regardless of their financial circumstances.

There are other new business models emerging in Indian healthcare. One of these schemes is converting online search queries to business opportunities by offering elective surgeries to those patients searching for them on the internet. The ones who run such operations do not own a hospital but instead lease hospital infrastructure and then hire doctors and medical equipment to carry out the surgeries. An unfortunate case in Mumbai last year highlighted the perils of this model.[4]

Runa Handa was a 47-year-old, single mother who worked at a bank in Mumbai. She had opted for a weight-loss procedure through one such online business entity. An executive from the startup contacted her with the details of the procedure, which involved the insertion of an intragastric balloon. The next day, she received a prescription on WhatsApp from the company in which a general surgeon, a proctologist and a laparoscopic surgeon suggested that she undergo a bariatric therapy because her Body Mass Index (BMI) met the minimum mandated by India's insurance regulator for such a procedure to be covered.

The prescribed treatment's estimated cost was about ₹4 lakh, involving the patient swallowing a pill that inflates into a balloon once inside the stomach. This limits the amount of food a person can eat and causes a calorie deficit, resulting in weight loss. The procedure was carried out at a hospital in Mumbai's Goregaon suburb. However, about half an hour later, Runa began to feel uneasy. In pain, she started vomiting. Despite requesting the doctors to remove the capsule from her stomach, she was counselled that the uneasiness and nausea is a normal reaction to the procedure. Her situation continued to deteriorate over the next few days. Five days after the procedure, she passed away, leaving behind a four-year-old son. Her death is now the subject matter of a police inquiry.

This case was quoted in a petition moved a few months later by Dr Malpani in the Supreme Court that asked for checks on 'illegal advertising' by corporate hospitals in which digital marketing, pushy sales executives and discount offers all try to convert consulting outpatients into surgical inpatients. It called this emerging model 'healthcare on venture capital steroids'. The petition argued that allowing private hospitals to issue advertisements unfettered by the kind of regulations that bind individual practitioners skews the market in their favour. Dr Malpani's lawyer says that the matter is still under consideration in the Supreme Court.

While individual doctors come under the purview of the NMC Act, 2019, corporate hospitals are governed by the rules of the Clinical Establishments Act (Registration and Regulation) Act, 2010. With the rules framed under the NMC Act having been kept in abeyance, individual medical practitioners are governed by the Indian Medical Council (Professional Conduct, Etiquette and Ethics) Regulations, 2002, which state that soliciting of patients, directly or indirectly, by a physician or by institutions or organisations is unethical.[5] It adds that a physician must not make use of any form of advertising or publicity through any mode, either alone or with others, to invite attention to them or to their professional position, skill, qualification, achievements, attainments, specialities, appointments, associations, affiliations or honours. All those things now appear routinely in advertisements issued by private hospitals.

Lost in translation

Translation in medicine refers to the inclusion of recent scientific concepts into treatment modalities to ensure patients get the best of emerging science instead of having to wait for it to clear all regulatory requirements. In some situations, this expedited process can be a lifesaver. In 2012, Emily Whitehead, 6, became the first paediatric patient to receive chimeric antigen receptor T-cell therapy (CAR-T). It genetically engineers immune cells from the patient to make them attack the cancerous cells in the body. She was also the first patient with acute lymphoblastic leukaemia (ALL) to receive it. It saved her life.

It is, however, tricky territory. A resident doctor at a corporate hospital recalls an incident from a few years ago, when a seminar had been organised in his hospital on stem cell therapy. An outside 'expert' had been invited to make a presentation. When the expert was talking about what they claimed was a cure for type 2 diabetes using a kind of regenerative therapy, a senior consultant walked in to interrupt the talk. The resident doctor reminisces: 'The expert was talking about what they claimed was a cure for type 2 diabetes using a kind of regenerative therapy that is used for many other conditions but not for diabetes. The senior doctor stood in the middle of the seminar room and yelled, "Who invited this fraud?" There was sudden silence while the consultant continued to question the external expert about their education. He said that there is no evidence of the intervention working for type 2 diabetes, and he knew it because he went to one of the top three institutions in the world for that discipline and was one of the people who had framed the guidelines. Having said his piece, the consultant stormed out after accusing the others at the hospital of corrupting the minds of young doctors with information that had no scientific basis. Through all of this, the staff of the external expert kept distributing pamphlets among the audience', the resident recalls. 'The 'expert' too was unfazed, and the senior who had called out the external expert sat peaceably in his chair showing no signs of perturbation.'

It was a rare instance of a doctor speaking up against his own fraternity, albeit in a closed medical forum. A top endocrinologist at a corporate institute admits that there are instances of 'absolute quackery' being offered to diabetes patients in the name of cutting-edge medicine, but it is difficult to call these people out because it is a pervasive network in which there are 'friends' and 'friends of friends' and thus it can get ugly. Many such therapies with limited evidentiary backing are sold with tall promises and high prices. Patients are left with nowhere to go to seek redress when the results do not match the hype.

This is particularly true of recalcitrant diseases or chronic conditions in which medication and lifestyle changes are required for the rest of the patient's life. Self-proclaimed pioneers and miracle makers offer relief or cures for debilitating conditions that make the patient and their family very vulnerable. Such individuals and companies had become hyperactive during the COVID-19 pandemic, when so-called miracle cures were endorsed by ministers. But their activities are not limited to any particular disease or public health emergency. Some have been exposed by media investigations yet continue their scams unhindered because the government is reluctant to intervene. Vigilant professionals often take to social media to call out instances of unproven medicine being promoted as panacea.

An online spat broke out in 2024 between two individuals from vastly different walks of life: one, a star with a massive fan following not just in the Tamil and Telugu film audiences but also nationally; the other, a doctor and activist from Kerala, whose strident opposition to the propagation of unscientific solutions in the name of traditional medicine earned him the wrath of many, the suspension of his social media account and an ongoing litigation. The face-off was ugly but perhaps warranted, given the number of celebrities who, by sharing 'advice' without context or qualification, unwittingly end up being brand ambassadors of medical procedures with little or no scientific basis.

In early July 2024, actress Samantha Ruth Prabhu wrote on Instagram about an 'alternative approach' to fighting off a common cold by nebulising oneself with a mixture of hydrogen peroxide and distilled water. Nebulising is a process that turns liquid medicine into a mist that can be inhaled. Prabhu added a photo of herself that showed her inhaling something through a mask from a bottle of transparent liquid. 'Works like magic,' she added. 'Avoid unnecessary use of tablets.'[6]

The 'magical' solution she advocated is a commonly used disinfectant. It is a corrosive compound used in medical establishments for deep cleaning. During the COVID-19 pandemic, among many other offbeat remedies for the virus that still did not have a cure, there was a trend of using hydrogen peroxide in nebulising machines. Doctors were alarmed, and the Asthma and Allergy Foundation of America quickly moved to issue a statement warning that hydrogen peroxide can cause tissue damage if one swallows it or breathes it in.

True to his take-no-prisoners advocacy style, the activist-doctor Cyriac Abby Philips – better known by his social media moniker 'The Liver Doc' – blasted Prabhu in an online response, calling her a 'health and science illiterate' as he referenced the American Foundation's warning to make his point. Dr Philips added that in 'a rational and scientifically progressive society', this woman would be 'charged with endangering public health and fined or put behind bars' and called on India's health ministry 'or any health regulatory body' to do something about these social-media stars 'damaging public health'.[7] He challenged the authorities by asking if they would instead choose to 'remain spineless and let people die'.[8] The exchange lasted for a couple of days on social media and ended with Dr Philips targeting Prabhu's doctor instead of her.

Dr Philips is one of the few individuals from within the medical profession who have taken it upon themselves to debunk misinformation and prevent patients from falling prey to their propagation and misuse by unethical professionals. But the problem of celebrities becoming role models or advocates for unscientific or inappropriate health interventions resurfaces frequently. Indian celebrities are not the only ones who may wittingly, or otherwise, exert irrational influence over patient choices. The most famous instance of this is from 2013, when Hollywood star Angelina Jolie announced that she had undergone a double mastectomy (removal of both breasts) as a preventive measure against breast cancer.

The disease had already claimed her mother's life, and at the time of the announcement, her aunt too had been stricken by breast cancer. The latter died a few months later. Jolie's physicians diagnosed that she had a mutation in one of her genes that made her more likely than others to get both breast and ovarian cancer – a disease that her grandmother had succumbed to. However, the most striking fallout of Jolie's decision was not necessarily medical.

Since times immemorial, a woman's breasts have been inexorably associated with her beauty. Hearing that one of the most beautiful women in the world had voluntarily had hers removed was encouraging for millions of women around the world who have had to undergo the same procedure as a life-saving measure following a cancer diagnosis. Doctors, families and patients all used the example of Angelina Jolie to normalise a very difficult and painful decision. The news also had a positive impact on awareness about genetic testing for cancer.[9]

However, celebrity choices, no matter how influential, are not accurate inputs for a healthcare decision. Neither is mainstream news media, with its own biases and information limitation, the best proponent of science. An analysis of media reporting of Jolie's decision in Canada, the United Kingdom and the United States found that the coverage focused on the 'courageous' nature of her decision while ignoring the rarity of her condition.[10] A study conducted in the United Kingdom in 2021 found that rates for mastectomies in the 20 years prior to Jolie's announcement were at approximately 24 per cent but more than doubled to 51.8 per cent after her revelation.[11] The authors of the study warned clinicians to be aware of how 'media news can impact on the delivery of cancer-related services' and stated that communicating 'objective assessment of risk' is important 'when counselling women on the merits of risk-reducing surgery'.

In India too there was a spike in testing rates for the two genes mentioned by Jolie, despite the tests costing over ₹50,000. There were instances of double mastectomies reported as well.[12,13] The knee-jerk response caused concern among the medical fraternity. This is where an ethical practitioner could frame the conversation in the correct context, while an unethical one could use it as an opportunity. Doctors from the Tata Memorial Cancer Institute wrote in the *Indian Journal of Medical Ethics* that Jolie's choice was 'too drastic'.[14] They said that it was 'a matter of ethical duty' for doctors to present a less invasive treatment as an option to patients so that they could make an informed decision rather than rushing headlong into something based on decisions taken by somebody else.

When former Indian cricketer Navjot Singh Sidhu claimed that his wife had overcome stage four breast cancer by following a dietary regimen that 'starved' cancer and targeted it with turmeric and neem,[15] a couple of hundred doctors from Mumbai's Tata Memorial Hospital were concerned enough to issue a cautionary statement. They said that the retired cricketer's statements have 'no high-quality evidence to support them', pointing out that while research was ongoing for some of the mentioned products, there was 'no clinical data currently to recommend their use as anti-cancer agents'. The statement urged the public to 'not delay their treatment by following unproven remedies' but instead to consult a cancer specialist if they have any symptoms of cancer. 'Cancer is curable if detected early and proven treatments for cancer include surgery, radiation therapy and chemotherapy,' concluded the statement.[16]

Appropriate technology

The fine lines between medicine and quackery can be breached merely based on what intervention is being used for which condition. For example, hyperbaric oxygen therapy (HOT) – which involves breathing pure oxygen in a pressurised environment – is routinely used for treating combat injuries and is a very important treatment modality for military hospitals. However, certain corporate hospitals have also started offering it as a cutting-edge therapy for healing wounds to those who can afford to pay for it. Particular targets are patients with diabetic foot ulcers (DFU), which can take a very long time to heal and sometimes get infected.

In 2024, the American Diabetes Association issued a statement that despite great interest in this treatment to expedite healing of chronic DFUs, there has only been one positive randomised control trial report of increased healing rates.[17] More recent studies have failed to provide corroborating evidence. They pointed out that HOT should not be widely used for managing non-healing DFUs. Despite this, a HOT session at a corporate hospital in Delhi can cost up to ₹5,000.

Many other non-regular therapies such as bee-sting therapy for rheumatoid arthritis have gained traction in recent years. These therapies are offered at high prices to unsuspecting patients at corporate hospitals with a promise of dramatic results, despite deep reservations within sections of the medical community about the ethical connotations of doing so. The equipment for some of these therapies is very expensive, so once it has been procured by a hospital, doctors are under pressure to recover the cost as quickly as possible.

There are also therapies that are approved by the regulators and backed by solid evidence. The previously mentioned CAR-T that cured little Emily Whitehead now has a homegrown Indian version. NexCar 19, that was unveiled in 2024 by President Droupadi Murmu, costs $30,000 to 40,000 for a single session, which is a tenth of the cost at which CAR-T is available. These therapies work for blood cancers but may not work for some other types of the disease.

Doctors have a position of absolute authority when it comes to therapy choices, but the decision is not always purely clinical. A senior oncologist, who spent decades at one of the best government institutes in the country before joining the private sector, says: 'Some therapies are suitable for some diseases. Take the example of proton beam radiotherapy. The recommended use is only for paediatric brain tumours because of its precision. But doctors started pushing it for all cases, even those that could have been treated equally well with regular radiotherapy.'

The argument his colleagues used, he explains, was that the precision would minimise collateral tissue damage. He says: 'I would always say you do not need a machine gun to kill a housefly. The cost differential is massive – proton beam therapy could cost up to 90 per cent more than regular radiotherapy.' There are specific indications for the use of cutting-edge therapies. If doctors choose to ignore those for reasons other than professional discretion, there would be far-reaching ethical and economic implications.

Another aspect is the overuse of technology. Much like drugs, technology comes with some side effects. For example, many modern diagnostic and therapeutic equipment use radioactive or electromagnetic radiation that can cause damage to the body with overexposure. That is why X-rays are always conducted in specially insulated rooms, and the technician will wear a protective vest and move out of the room before using it. It is to protect themselves from the high levels of radiation exposure that their jobs require daily. For patients too this can be a concern which is why frequent radiation imaging decisions need to be taken clinically and judiciously.

An additional cause of concern is the increasing use of radiation-based diagnostic and therapeutic interventions for children; they are more vulnerable to ionising radiation than adults, because they are still growing. Cells in their body regenerate and divide faster than they do in adults, so it is risky to accelerate that growth by exposing them to radiation. Cancer is basically caused by unregulated multiplication of body cells. According to the National Cancer Institute in the United States, people who have had at least one CT scan before the age of 22 have an increased risk of developing haematological cancers, particularly lymphoid and myeloid cancers and acute leukaemia. In the 12 years after a single CT scan, the risk of cancer was about 1–2 cases for every 10,000 scans performed on children and young people.[18]

Unfortunately, in India there is poor awareness even among doctors about these downsides. A study was done among the doctors at AIIMS in Delhi to check their awareness about the hazards of radiation imaging. A hundred junior doctors – including senior residents, junior residents' research officers and interns from the departments of medicine, paediatrics and surgery – were asked to fill out a questionnaire. In the premiere tertiary care institute in the country, only about 27 per cent of respondents were correctly able to state the radiation exposure that occurs with a chest X-ray. For some of the other tests that utilise ionising radiation, which is potentially harmful to the patient if overused, the rate of correct response dropped to as low as 2 per cent.

One out of five respondents did not know that an ultrasound is not associated with ionising radiation and about one in three held the incorrect belief that an MRI uses ionising radiation. Overall, 32 per cent expressed a desire to know about the degree of exposure with each test and the risk associated with it. Interestingly, none of the doctors felt the need to provide patients with any information regarding radiation exposure, nor the need to get patient consent. These findings were discussed by pulmonary medicine expert Dr Randeep Guleria at an international workshop in Brussels in 2009. He later went on to become the director at AIIMS.[19]

One of the diseases most commonly linked to ionising radiation is cancer, a disease that we are becoming increasingly and uncomfortably familiar with. It is now well established that exposure to a CT scan is associated with an increased risk of cancer, with the risk depending on the part of the body scanned. The estimated risk of fatal cancers linked to CT scans is about one every 2,000 scans. The radiation exposure from three or four CT scans in adults is roughly equivalent to that experienced by atomic bomb survivors in Japan who were about 3 kilometres from ground zero at the time of detonation. In fact, a lot of the present-day understanding of the health risks of ionising radiation comes from long-term studies done on these survivors from Hiroshima and Nagasaki. However, emergency medicine physicians also argue that many more lives are saved by the information gained from these scans than are harmed by their side effects.

Medical science is not about the latest fads and gimmicks but about finding the appropriate treatment for an ailment, even if the solution is a couple of hundred years old. That is why cutting-edge therapies and medicines should be used with adequate clinical discretion. They are more expensive and also come with unknown risks that may emerge only when long-term data in patients starts being collated and analysed. Disinterested clinical judgement is the only defence against this, making medical ethics the last bastion standing between patients and corporate greed that can increase awareness about the known and unknown risks associated with technology overuse.

12

Acing the Playbook

Hospitals are daunting enough without the prospect of a health setback being concomitant with a financial one. Two silos – public and private institutions – comprise the Indian health system; the former symbolise accessibility and affordability and the latter bring world-class care into the country for anyone willing to pay the price. But it is neither feasible nor practical for the public sector to compensate for the questionable business practices of the private sector without attempting to infuse accountability and ethics into their functioning. There has not even been any serious attempt to direct consumer choices towards the more ethical practitioners.

Just like ethical doctors coexist with the unethical ones – much like in any other profession – so also there are hospitals with differing business mores and divergent goals. The problem for an ordinary person is how to distinguish the wheat from the chaff. Even though we live in the age of online reviews and social media ratings, they are not optimally used in healthcare. Each one of us probably knows more than one person with an unpleasant hospital experience.

Restaurant reviewer or food critic is a serious job description. Countless people the world over make a living out of it; that number exploded in recent years as social media made critics and influencers out of every person with a reasonably good camera, a stable internet connection and a few thousand followers. Top publications, both national and international, routinely publish a list of what they rate as the top restaurants. These are inputs that we keep in mind (besides affordability) when choosing the next dinner destination. A good review or an honourable mention in a popular column can trigger a significant, if transient, uptick in business for any eatery; even a roadside tea stall that features in a social media post will see increased customer footfall over the next few days. Reviews guide our choices when it comes to online shopping. We look at the number of 'stars' a product has, check the number of customers who have submitted their opinions and read reviews by verified users before making our choice of which air fryer to buy. But we do not have access to similar insights when we are trying to decide where to go for medical treatment. This is ironical because healthcare choices are fundamental to the right to life. The only option we have there is to fly blind because authenticated, neutral and reliable reviews of healthcare professionals and institutions, based either on their competence or the ethics and affordability of the medicine they practise, are not available.

Negligence in healthcare cannot be compared with a poor meal at a restaurant or a defective online purchase. Thousands in India die because of unregulated, inaccessible healthcare every year, while another few thousand face impoverishment because of catastrophic health expenses. That is why this gap in feedback is appalling.[1]

When it comes to reviews of private hospitals and doctors, a few anonymous reviews – easily rigged – on a handful of websites is all we have access to. Many of these websites charge a small fee from doctors and hospitals to feature them. Some also provide add-on services such as managing online appointments. There is a clear and acknowledged business relationship between the two; so the sites stand to lose clients – doctors and hospitals – should they allow negative reviews to be published. They do not owe anything to the end user – the patient – and have no obligation to supply them with an honest assessment of these service providers.

So, the patient must go by word-of-mouth reputations of doctors and hospitals or is attracted to well-known names or brands. Occasionally they are swayed by media reports or by advertisements, usually about the availability of latest medical technology or the movement of a reputed consultant to a hospital closer to home.

Not even the ambitious Ayushman Bharat Digital Mission, which aims to create a digital health infrastructure in the country, complete with a comprehensive registry of verified medical professionals, has a rating system that would help patients choose better. The registry is in a fledgling state.

Does the Indian patient then not have any option but to be completely in the power of doctors and hospitals whose ethical compass or professional competence or both may be suspect? There is nothing to pre-empt this now.

But there may be some ways to better negotiate India's private healthcare space. They may not be game changers, but these small precautions can perhaps make the hospital experience a little less trying.

Seeking information is your right

Most Indian doctors do not like knowledgeable patients because they ask too many questions and treat doctors not as deities but as just another professional who has a duty to explain their actions. Be that patient. Read up about the condition you are suffering from, the treatment options available, the side effects that may be encountered and the possible complications. This is not as easy as it sounds because the internet is also a minefield of misinformation with few filters. The diagnosis options that you encounter if you search for the causes of headache will also include brain tumour. There is no need to jump to the most ominous diagnosis; if you do, you will play into the hands of corporate healthcare, because a scared patient is the perfect grist for that mill. It exploits patient anxiety, so refrain from reaching a conclusion about your condition just from online research. Let your doctor do their job, while you continue to push their boundaries, seeking information that you need to reassure yourself, including about alternate diagnoses, treatment options and the pros and cons of each of those. If your doctor seems uncomfortable answering your questions, change your doctor.

In 2019, the National Human Rights Commission and the ministry of health and family welfare released a Charter of Patient Rights.[2] The first of those rights is the right to information. The charter declares that every patient has a right to adequate and relevant information about the nature and cause of the illness, a provisional or confirmed diagnosis, proposed investigations and management and possible complications, to be explained at their level of understanding in a language they know. The treating physician has a duty to communicate this information in person or depute qualified assistants to do so.

An accurate estimate of the cost of treatment and evidence as to why it is the recommended approach is also included in this essential information. It is the duty of the hospital management to communicate this information in writing to the patient. They should also be similarly informed about any additional costs that could be incurred due to changes in the physical condition of the patient or the line of treatment. On completion of treatment, the patient has the right to receive an itemised bill and to receive an explanation for each item regardless of the source or the mode of payment and to receive receipts for any payments made.

It is also the right of the patient to know the identity and professional status of not just the primary physician they have been admitted under, but also that of the various care providers (including nurses, ward boys and other staff) in the hospital. The hospital management has a duty to provide this information in writing routinely to all patients and their families. Therefore, do not hesitate to ask for the information that you need.

Soon after PMJAY was launched, Dr Aniruddha Malpani had petitioned the government to incorporate an element of what he calls 'information therapy' into the programme to help patients make more informed choices. He defines the concept as 'the right information to the right person at the right time'. He is yet to hear from the government on this proposal.

Around the world, there are several initiatives that help patients make choices based on evidence. One of them called

'Choosing Wisely' lists five essential questions that patients should ask their doctors. These are: How essential is the procedure or treatment? What are the risks? What are the Costs? What are the alternatives? What happens if they choose not to do it? It is important to understand the difference between essential and non-essential procedures before committing to anything.

Check what the package does and does not include

The stress of a hospital admission can make it easy to gloss over seemingly unimportant details, and few read through the admission form carefully before signing it. Nor is it commonplace to seek exhaustive information on the inclusions and exclusions under the room rent or package, in case that is what is on offer for you. Some hospitals have started charging separately for meals, oxygen, special mattresses and even towels used for sponging the patient. It may be better to clarify these things beforehand rather than go into a long-drawn dispute over the bill later. Packages usually do not account for any complications, including the simplest, almost inevitable ones that may occur in a large proportion of patients. There is no room either for differing rates of recovery. Anything excluded can have a significant bearing on the bill as it may need a lengthier hospitalisation that would then be billed outside of the package. Spend time understanding the potential repercussions of these exclusions at the time of admission.

The first response when preparing for surgery is usually to check for insurance approvals. But equally important is to check which doctor you are going to be admitted under. It seems like a mundane detail that few pay attention to, but it is important because in some institutions if your primary doctor is not your surgeon, you might end up paying a premium on your final bill as a sort of an incentive to the physician for referring you for a surgical procedure.

The reasons for this practice are explained elsewhere in this book. Being admitted under the surgeon instead of the clinician will ensure that you do not end up paying for a part of that 'incentive'. If your clinician is somebody you trust and would prefer that they take a more active role in your treatment decisions, you can always request them to visit during your hospitalisation. Few surgeons would object to that. That way you would just pay for a few visitation charges, which would be a lot less than paying for a larger sum linked to the surgery.

Take nothing and nobody for granted

Continue to ask questions and be vigilant through the duration of the treatment. It may be difficult as a patient, so have your family member or attendant do it for you. It is important to keep very close track of the medicines being prescribed and administered, the equipment that are being used or not used, the samples being collected and the doctors who are visiting. Medicines can be difficult to track because they are usually administered by nurses. However, most medicines are kept near the patient's bed so make sure you are familiar with each one. It is a good way to also keep track of doctors' visits, particularly the ones who have been given a referral. If the medicines they prescribed are no longer being used, their visits may not be essential either. Do not fall into a false sense of security with the assumption that visits by many doctors automatically translate into the best care. But they certainly translate into bigger bills. Every time a doctor's signature appears on the patient's file, a visitation charge is due to them. If the visits do not seem essential, quiz the doctor about why they are needed. If possible, also keep a close watch and a written count of the samples collected and sent for tests and whether all the reports have been attached to the file.

All these things will need to be crosschecked at the time of billing. If a machine is prescribed as 'SOS' and kept by the bed but never actually used, the standard practice is to presume constant use and charge accordingly. This can and should be contested at the time of discharge, and it is important to forcefully make the point that this is an unfair trade practice that will not stand the test of regulatory scrutiny should the matter be escalated. Corporate hospitals sometimes do back down if countered on legitimate points where they know they are in the wrong and they see a real possibility of the patient taking it to the media. This is because a little discount for them is a small price to avert bad publicity. The threat of even a social media post may be enough. Many of the biggest revelations about questionable corporate practices have happened through such posts.[3]

There is another reason why vigilance is constantly required. Standards of nursing care can ebb and flow in Indian hospitals. Nurses in most private institutions are poorly paid and have to work long hours, so there is a very high attrition rate in the nursing workforce with trained and experienced professionals moving abroad, where Indian nursing staff is in very high demand. They are constantly replaced by fresh graduates. It is therefore very important for attendants, especially of patients who are seriously ill, to keep track of basic nursing chores such as cleaning of the feeding tubes or administration of injectable drugs. A doctor shares a story about how potentially devastating the effects of poorly trained nursing staff can be. He was on night duty and writing a drug chart standing near the nurses' station. 'A young nurse, in all earnestness, came to ask whether she should administer subcutaneous heparin (an anticoagulation agent) through the IV cannula that was already inserted into a patient,' he recalls. 'She said that the patient did not want another prick and had asked her to just push it through the cannula.' The doctor froze hearing her question. Heparin is administered subcutaneously to ensure slow absorption. Pushing it into the blood vessel would have caused major bleeding in the patient. He told her: 'You did a good job by asking, please continue doing that.' When she left, he asked the nursing in-charge to send the girl for a training immediately.

A common practice in many private hospitals is to deny access to the patient file until the time of discharge. However, patients have a right to access it at any point they want to, including to review test reports or to photograph them to send for a second opinion. Do not let anyone at any hospital tell you otherwise.

Consider buying/renting small medical equipment

Rarely do patients go into the hospital expecting to stay there for a long time. But there are circumstances that demand prolonged hospitalisation, and one such situation is when a patient needs 24/7 monitoring. If such a contingency arises, consider buying your own equipment, particularly the small ones such as a glucometer which many of us already use at home. For many such common tests, hospitals bill by pricks – so every time a nurse comes to collect your sample to record a blood sugar reading, there will be an entry in the bill. Over a long period this can be a tidy sum. If you already have an oxygen cylinder at home, consider taking it to the hospital. The clinical and the billing departments of the hospital run parallel to each other, so the billing meter literally starts running the moment the hospital rolls one of its own cylinders into the ward, irrespective of whether it has been used or not. Patients who have devices such as a DVT pump or a bipap machine at home would also do well to take them to the hospital if they need it regularly.

In case a machine is not available, check if it is possible for you to rent from outside the hospital. That would come cheaper as hospitals add a markup to even the equipment they take on rent. You might have no option but to pay for bigger and more expensive equipment such as ventilators. But the small savings can add up. It is not standard practice for hospitals to allow people to bring their own equipment, but there is no actual rule against it so it may be good to initiate this conversation either with the treating doctor or the floor manager. Ask also to buy medicine from chemists outside and not from the hospital pharmacy.

There are multiple directives that clearly lay down that corporate hospitals cannot force patients to buy medicines from in-house pharmacies. In 2014, the National Consumer Disputes Redressal Commission had specifically stated this.[4] Then in 2022, Maharashtra Food and Drug Administration (FDA) also issued a notification that reiterated this same principle.[5] There were discussions at various points to bring in regulations about this, but they did not come to fruition.

The most common pushback to this request is about the quality of medicines, but you can argue that you would buy the same brands available in the in-house pharmacy. It is not easy for the patients to broach this topic with their doctor, because there are concerns that any strident position may be construed as disrespectful. But the resultant savings can be significant. Many corporate hospitals have several chemist shops in their vicinity that, in a bid to outdo each other, actually offer larger discounts than available anywhere else in the same city. Attendants just need to step out of the hospital premises to buy most medicines at a bargain price.

You could also ask to get some diagnostic tests done from outside the hospital. This may not be feasible for tests requiring large equipment and may even be problematic from the sample collection perspective, since hospitals can cite security as the reason to not let a technician from a different laboratory enter the premises. But make the request and persist. If the hospital does agree, call up the laboratory and try to bargain. This is easier than you think, particularly if you maintain that you have not been referred by a doctor but have decided to get the tests done of your own accord. That means the doctor's commission, which would be factored into the listed price, would not need to be paid by the lab, and many establishments are willing to pass that discount on to the customer.

Tell the clinical team to be mindful of costs

Inflated hospital bills in the private sector are sometimes the result of structural flaws in the way the management does business and the way some doctors practise their medicine. There is one set of doctors who, at the back of every clinical decision, are also trying to keep a record of the circumstances in which it was taken so they can be defended in a court of law, if needed. The trust deficit between patients and doctors has led to a vicious circle. But candour can help to win the doctor's trust as their natural instincts are still to help the patient, regardless of how much room for that has shrunk in the corporate setup in the last few decades. Coming clean with the clinical team on financial constraints can also ease conversations about which tests are essential and which are not. Doctors can then also understand that many of your questions stem from financial concern rather than any doubts about their clinical competence. So, they do not need to get defensive and can skip some unnecessary tests. One important caveat: refrain from quoting a maximum spending capacity. This might be counterproductive. If the bill is less than your stated limit, there might be attempts by a hospital to push it closer to that number.

There is a term very commonly used in hospitals – LAMA or leave against medical advice. This is an option that you can exercise at any point after understanding the implications and precautions involved with taking the patient home or to a different medical establishment. In case there are suspicions of a hospital trying to keep a patient for reasons other than medical, this option can come in very handy.

When offered a day procedure, compare hourly charges to the price for an overnight stay

It is comforting to not have to spend a night at a hospital. That is why when given the option of a same-day procedure, the lure of being back home by the evening makes us immediately jump at it. Don't rush into this decision without comparing the costs with an overnight hospitalisation. For day procedures, room rent is charged by the hour. Even if you stay for half a day, you may end up paying more than what you would have for a full day. While an overnight room rent may be upwards of ₹5,000, the per hour rate could easily be ₹1,200 to ₹1,500, which means even a five-hour stay could be comparatively costlier. Many insurance companies do not cover day procedures. It may seem reasonable to pay out of pocket if the estimated cost is something you can afford, but you might then end up paying more than the insurance provider would pay for the same treatment. This is because they negotiate favourable rate contracts with hospitals that are not applicable for individual patients not availing the insurance cover.

If you are advised hospitalisation for a longer period, it may be a smarter idea to share a room instead of taking a single room. That is because all charges – big ones such as surgery fees and small ones like for consumables – increase in proportion to the room rent. It is a controversial business practice that has survived much criticism. Thus, when opting for a single room you will pay for much more than just the difference in room rates – almost every item on the bill will be proportionately costlier. Billing practices too are evolving rapidly; previously, doctors would give an earlier discharge time in the notes to ensure the patient is not billed for an additional day. But administrative oversight in billing now ensures that this can no longer be done; many hospitals have now started to bill for a full day if the three-hour grace period for insurance clearance is breached.

Be cautious about experimental or non-indicated therapies

The lure of a miracle cure is powerful, but the pull is even stronger when the illness is chronic or one with limited treatment options. That is the vulnerability that some hospitals and unethical practitioners take advantage of when peddling experimental therapies. Sometimes they will advise therapies that have been proven to be effective in diseases other than the one for which it is being advised. These are known as non-indicated therapies. A therapy or an intervention should only be used for conditions for which there is evidence (papers published in peer reviewed journals) that they work. To use it for something else is like putting a person with a thyroid hormone deficiency on insulin. Both are hormones, but they perform different functions within the body, and so one cannot be the replacement for another! While insulin will work for some diabetics – for them it is an indicated therapy – it will do nothing for hypothyroidism, which is a deficiency of the thyroid hormone.

No matter how fantastic the promise of succour, do not opt for such a therapy unless all established and traditional options have been exhausted. This is not to say that all experimental therapies are problematic. Translational medicine has emerged as a thriving medical discipline in recent years with a very strong focus on interdisciplinary collaborations.

But the decision needs to be taken with a complete understanding of the pros and cons. It is important to have trust in the doctor advocating it, but that alone cannot be the deciding factor. Ask for medical literature on the topic and read at least the abstract, the results and the discussion sections of the published papers to get a sense of what it would entail. However, as we are not experts who can weigh and dissect the advice given by a professional, taking a second or even a third professional opinion is the prudent thing to do instead of trusting just one person blindly. If you do decide to opt for a therapy that is still being tested, remember that you are basically agreeing to be part of a clinical trial. So, do not pay for the therapy.

Subjects in a clinical trial do not pay because they are offering themselves up to test whether the treatment works and are also subjecting themselves to its yet unknown side effects, which could potentially even be fatal. You should consider yourself as part of a research project, the expenses of which are covered by the sponsor – most likely the pharmaceutical company that has developed the product being used for the therapy. In fact, you might even be entitled to compensation for your time and the risks you take in being part of a clinical trial.

Scrutinise your bill

When your treatment is complete and you are feeling better, you probably can't wait to finally go home. But there is one crucial step left. This is the time to take a metaphorical magnifying glass and scrutinise the bill thoroughly. This should ideally be done before it is sent to your insurance provider. Were all the listed medicines administered? Did the nutritionist do as many visits as they charged for? Some of the scrutiny of the clinical decisions would happen at the insurance company's level before the clearances come, and that is one of the parameters that are used to decide the amount to be approved for payment. However, they might not know as much as you do about what went down inside the hospital, which is why you should ask for a copy of the bill in advance.

This is also the time to pull out that carefully maintained count of doctor visits and sample collections and see if it matches up. There may be a few times when the doctor just signed the file without entering the room and checking on the patient. Flag those and get them removed.

Also, ensure that the discharge papers include the reports of all the tests that have been billed. If you have been charged for three blood sugar tests, then you should be given all three reports. If not, contest the charge. This is also the time to bring up anything that may have gone wrong during the hospitalisation – a faulty cannula insertion, delayed response from the nurse or doctor, surgical complications – as they can help negotiate a discount.

After discharge, make sure to check whether any of the follow-up checks are covered in the package that you had opted for. Preserve every document from the hospitalisation, including prescriptions, test reports and invoices. These are important as medical records; they also help make sure that the hospital can be held accountable if any complications arise in the future.

Almost every person that leaves a hospital after spending a few days hopes to never have to come back. Many people go back ever grateful to the doctor; it is still a very common sight in Indian hospitals where patients or their family members touch the doctor's feet. But in very few cases is the discharge from the hospital a completely stress-free affair. This book may perhaps make it a little less so, one hospitalisation at a time, so that you can concentrate on recovering instead of fretting about how much the illness set you back financially.

Get well soon.

Postscript

Post COVID-19, the Indian healthcare sector has been booming with investors keen to pump in more money. The going has never been so good for the industry. The private investment coming into the sector should benefit the Indian patient. It is a space that has enormous room and an urgent need to grow to be able to cater to our country's vast population. The number of people the sector employs is a staggering 7.5 million, according to one report,[1] making it one of the largest employers in the country. As the supply side is strengthened through the establishment of more medical and paramedical training institutes, the infusion of liquidity will reduce the time lag in technological breakthroughs reaching Indian hospitals. This in turn will fuel the demand for a skilled workforce. So, these numbers are expected to grow significantly every year.

The private sector is almost always the first to bring in emerging medical technologies to the country. Government institutions, outside of the elite AIIMS and PGIMER, may take years to get their hands on the same equipment and then sometimes fail to use them optimally when they do get it. Therefore, how private hospitals deploy the latest technology can become the difference between life and death for many patients. This is why there are intermittent conversations about health technology assessment (HTA). Influx of investment should ideally benefit the Indian patient, giving them more options for affordable and accessible healthcare. But the experience so far with the private sector has been of reduced affordability. Healthcare inflation in India is more than double the retail inflation. Businesses must care about bottom lines but that cannot be the sole benchmark.

The instances of corporate business practices and medical decision-making processes highlighted in this book are not the only ways hospitals nurture bottom lines; there are newer ways emerging every day. A hospital may also choose not to indulge in any of the practices that this book highlights and implement a non-exploitative business model. Indeed, many doctors continue to practise ethical medicine in the corporate sector, while others have left it, unable to cope with the pressures and demands of a system that has different priorities than what they were taught in medical school. Policymakers are not unaware of the principles and the pitfalls of corporate healthcare. Political will is deficient but not without reason. However, regulatory oversight has not been a policy priority unless mandated by judicial interventions.

Perhaps this is because corporate healthcare caters to a class of people who are notoriously reluctant voters. The perception among the political class also is that provision for accessible and affordable healthcare is not an election winner in the way a monthly stipend or a free bicycle may be.

Years ago, one politician from Haryana had told me about his disappointment that the 100-bed hospital that he had worked hard to establish in his constituency to reduce dependency on PGIMER, Chandigarh, resonated very little with his voters. They felt more excited about the proverbial *bijli-sadak-pani* (electricity, roads and water). This reality automatically pushes health way down in the list of political priorities. Even though a slew of government insurance schemes catering to the poorest social strata have been rolled out in recent years, regulating the private sector remains an academic discussion. It needs to move beyond that domain of discussion in the coming years, paving the way for the eventual rollout of universal health coverage in India that has public–private partnership as one of the pillars. If this book ends up playing a small part in that, it would have been worth the effort.

I would like to profusely thank the doctors and other individuals associated with private hospitals for laying bare the complications and the intricacies of intra-hospital processes in the spirit of transparency and accountability. I would also like to thank my editors, particularly former editor-in-chief at Bloomsbury, Krishan Chopra, for conceiving this book.

Notes

Introduction

1 https://www.livelaw.in/top-stories/supreme-court-disparity-health-care-costs-centre-standard-rates-clinical-establishment-act-250776
2 https://dashboard.pmjay.gov.in/pmj/#/
3 https://www.forbes.com/advisor/in/health-insurance/health-insurance-statistics/
4 https://www.niti.gov.in/sites/default/files/2023-02/Health-Insurance-for-India%E2%80%99s-Missing-Middle_08-12-2021.pdf

1 The MRP Trap

1 https://www.hindustantimes.com/delhi-news/gurgaon-s-fortis-hospital-bills-family-for-660-syringes-and-2-700-gloves-nadda-promises-action/story-dorjF5EaqC01ePLYUiS0fJ.html
2 https://timesofindia.indiatimes.com/city/gurgaon/parents-billed-rs-16l-for-7-year-olds-dengue-treatment-now-medanta-on-govts-radar/articleshow/62215241.cms
3 https://www.thehindu.com/news/cities/Delhi/father-withdraws-complaint-medanta-refunds-15-lakh/article23386460.ece
4 https://www.theweek.in/news/biz-tech/2018/02/22/private-hospitals-delhi-ncr-use-inflated-bills-overcharge-patients-nppa.html
5 https://cms.nic.in/ncdrcusersWeb/GetJudgement.do?method=GetJudgement&caseidin=0%2F0%2FRP%2F2448%2F2013&dtofhearing=2014-07-22
6 https://www.cci.gov.in/antitrust/orders/details/215/0
7 https://www.cci.gov.in/antitrust/orders/details/1013/0
8 https://indianlawwatch.com/max-fortis-apollo-and-other-big-hospital-chains-have-been-overcharging-patients-cci-investigation/
9 High Court of Delhi w.p.(c) 13588/2022 & Cm Appl. 41395/2022 Max Healthcare Vs CCI
10 https://www.businesstoday.in/industry/pharma/story/nppa-blames-four-delhi-hospitals-for-preferring-high-cost-medicines-over-price-controlled-ones-100836-2018-02-20

11 (2009) 163 DLT 319 (DB)
12 https://www.pharmabiz.com/NewsDetails.aspx?aid=161170&sid=2
13 https://pharmaceuticals.gov.in/sites/default/files/UCPMP%202024%20for%20website.pdf
14 https://web.stanford.edu/~jay/health_class/Readings/Lecture01/arrow.pdf
15 https://publicity.delhi.gov.in/publicity/chief-minister-directs-immediate-availability-medicines-delhi-government-hospitals-23rd
16 https://indiankanoon.org/doc/190673265/#:~:text=Hospitals%20should%20maintain%20a%20minimum%20inventory%20of,due%20time%20to%20ensure%20that%20there%20is
17 https://cag.gov.in/uploads/media/Report-No-17-of-2022-PA-on-CGHS-English-PDF-A-062f0e5d1382fa5-21939167-06343df4e4e7278-23942165.pdf
18 https://www.business-standard.com/india-news/govt-orders-cbi-probe-into-substandard-medicine-supply-in-delhi-hospitals-124010500953_1.html
19 https://www.business-standard.com/article/companies/aspirin-vanishes-from-drug-store-shelves-101090301008_1.html
20 https://timesofindia.indiatimes.com/india/after-price-control-several-key-drugs-in-short-supply/articleshow/45499903.cms

2 One Surgery for the Price of Two

1 https://www.outlookmoney.com/insurance/health-insurance/surge-pricing-in-healthcare-burdens-patients-and-insurers-as-hospitals-lay-peak-charges#:~:text=Just%20like%20how%20surge%20pricing,of%20a%20single%20comprehensive%20package.
2 https://economictimes.indiatimes.com/industry/banking/finance/insure/patients-insurers-feel-the-pain-as-hospitals-take-to-surge-pricing/articleshow/114195592.cms?from=mdr
3 https://jamanetwork.com/journals/jama/fullarticle/2760720#:~:text=%E2%80%9CSurprise%E2%80%9D%20billing%20occurs%20when,%2Dof%2Dnetwork%E2%80%9D)%20and
4 https://bmjopen.bmj.com/content/bmjopen/3/6/e002844.full.pdf
5 https://pubmed.ncbi.nlm.nih.gov/28400359/
6 https://dashboard.pmjay.gov.in/pmj/#/
7 https://www.sciencedirect.com/science/article/pii/S2213398420300816
8 https://dashboard.pmjay.gov.in/pmj/#/cghs
9 https://www.bloomberg.com/news/articles/2023-08-31/doctors-ghost-patients-charge-for-surgeries-left-to-residents
10 https://timesofindia.indiatimes.com/india/no-insurance-be-ready-to-pay-more-at-hospitals/articleshow/109657934.cms

3 The 'Package' Deal

1 https://www.mha.gov.in/sites/default/files/2022-09/MHARelease%25201962020_0%5B1%5D.pdf
2 https://www.deccanherald.com/business/health-insurance-understanding-room-rent-limit-is-crucial-1199525.html
3 https://www.deccanherald.com/business/health-insurance-understanding-room-rent-limit-is-crucial-1199525.html
4 https://timesofindia.indiatimes.com/toi-plus/health/are-heart-patients-getting-stents-they-dont-need/articleshow/115702565.cms
5 https://jamanetwork.com/journals/jamainternalmedicine/fullarticle/1108733#:~:text=Of%20the%20total%20649%20deaths,%2D1.16)%20(P%20%3D%20.
6 https://timesofindia.indiatimes.com/india/one-in-3-stent-implants-in-india-is-possibly-unnecessary/articleshow/57071863.cms#:~:text=Several%20senior%20cardiologists%20in%20India,turn%20out%20to%20be%20needless.
7 https://www.livemint.com/industry/manufacturing/stent-makers-and-importers-allowed-to-hike-prices-11714972812691.html
8 https://nmji.in/view-pdf/?article=fd50ac9ce37d20d548d8738c64e2314bgTEAHPnHQn8=

4 The Hidden Costs

1 https://irdai.gov.in/document-detail?documentId=394530
2 https://economictimes.indiatimes.com/industry/banking/finance/insure/patients-insurers-feel-the-pain-as-hospitals-take-to-surge-pricing/articleshow/114195592.cms?from=mdr
3 https://sansad.in/getFile/loksabhaquestions/annex/16/AU4000.pdf?source=pqals
4 https://sansad.in/getFile/loksabhaquestions/annex/16/AU4000.pdf?source=pqals
5 https://www.plumhq.com/corporate-health-report-2023
6 http://wbcerc.gov.in/cms/order
7 https://cms.nic.in/ncdrcusersWeb/GetJudgement.do?method=GetJudgement&caseidin=0%2F0%2FRP%2F1653%2F2016&dtofhearing=2023-10-12
8 https://www.sciencedirect.com/science/article/pii/S2213398420300725
9 https://www.niti.gov.in/sites/default/files/2021-12/AIIMS_STUDY_1.pdf
10 http://164.100.60.133/misc/draft%20cars/D3C-C12.pdf

5 To Refer or Not to Refer

1 http://wbcerc.gov.in/cms/order (25-7-2024)
2 https://www.bmj.com/content/348/bmj.g3169
3 https://timesofindia.indiatimes.com/india/hospital-hoarding-stirs-honesty-debate/articleshow/59151830.cms
4 https://valueadded.in/wp-content/uploads/2024/06/Referral-guidelines.pdf
5 https://dghs.gov.in/Uploaddata/Referral%20policy%2062024.pdf

6 Monitoring Is a Money-Spinner

1 https://theprint.in/health/past-covid-peak-heres-how-govt-plans-to-keep-white-elephant-psa-oxygen-plants-up-running/903592/
2 https://timesofindia.indiatimes.com/city/kolkata/ai-powered-remote-monitoring-system-implemented-in-kolkata-private-hospitals/articleshow/110981180.cms

7 Emergencies Feed Bottom Lines

1 http://wbcerc.gov.in/cms/order (Complaint ID : INT/KOL/2024/089)
2 https://assets.aeaweb.org/asset-server/files/9442.pdf
3 https://www.ncbi.nlm.nih.gov/pmc/articles/PMC5818801/
4 https://www.ncbi.nlm.nih.gov/pmc/articles/PMC8628817/
5 https://main.icmr.nic.in/sites/default/files/whats_new/NEDL_revision150124.pdf
6 https://timesofindia.indiatimes.com/city/chandigarh/hospital-management-booked-for-overcharging/articleshow/97540011.cms
7 https://www.niti.gov.in/sites/default/files/2021-12/AIIMS_STUDY_1.pdf
7 https://pubmed.ncbi.nlm.nih.gov/31562720/#full-view-affiliation-1

8 'Do You Have Insurance?'

1 https://www.reuters.com/markets/deals/temasek-acquires-41-stake-indias-manipal-health-2023-04-10/
2 https://www.siliconindia.com/shownews/apollo-ties-up-with-singapore-group-for-hospital-in-kolkata-nid-21854-cid-3.html
3 https://pmc.ncbi.nlm.nih.gov/articles/PMC10857549/
4 https://qualitysafety.bmj.com/content/31/1/54
5 https://timesofindia.indiatimes.com/india/indias-doctor-population-ratio-1834-minister/articleshow/105930987.cms
6 https://timesofindia.indiatimes.com/india/indias-doctor-population-ratio-1834-minister/articleshow/105930987.cms

7 https://economictimes.indiatimes.com/news/india/nmc-issues-guidelines-to-identify-fake-patients-in-medical-college-inspections/articleshow/116135578.cms?from=mdr
8 https://economictimes.indiatimes.com/industry/services/education/rs-1-4-crore/year-for-mbbs-the-college-that-offers-indias-costliest-medical-degree/articleshow/102740659.cms?from=mdr
9 https://medicaldialogues.in/mdtv/medico-legal-update/delay-in-diagnosing-complications-after-bariatric-surgery-results-in-patient-death-ncdrc-directs-kolkata-hospital-doctors-to-pay-rs-75-lakh-129508
10 https://www.newindianexpress.com/cities/delhi/2024/Feb/17/sir-ganga-ram-hospital-fined-over-patient-death-says-it-will-study-order
11 https://www.bmj.com/content/364/bmj.l750
12 https://www.ncbi.nlm.nih.gov/pmc/articles/PMC3728884/
13 https://www.researchgate.net/publication/365410265_Defensive_Medicine_in_the_Context_of_the_Indian_Health_System
14 https://www.fogsi.org/wp-content/uploads/announcements/Guidelines-and-Reportings-of-Hysterectomies.pdf
15 The National Family Health Survey is a periodic assessment of India's health and nutrition parameters and widely regarded as the most comprehensive and updated source of data on family health
16 https://pmc.ncbi.nlm.nih.gov/articles/PMC7544137/#:~:text=3.1.&text=Also%2C%20Fig%202%20exhibits%20that,delivered%20at%20home%20or%20elsewhere.
17 https://www.thelancet.com/journals/lancet/article/PIIS0140-6736(18)31928-7/fulltext
18 https://www.fogsi.org/wp-content/uploads/announcements/Guidelines-and-Reportings-of-Hysterectomies.pdf
19 https://nha.gov.in/img/resources/HBP-2.2-manual.pdf
20 https://indianexpress.com/article/cities/ahmedabad/pmjay-beneficiaries-who-died-after-angioplasty-did-not-need-surgery-fir-9668787/
21 https://timesofindia.indiatimes.com/city/ahmedabad/2-die-after-unwarranted-angioplasty-in-pm-jay-scam-in-gandhinagar/articleshow/115280875.cms

9 Too Much of a Good Thing

1 https://economictimes.indiatimes.com/industry/healthcare/biotech/healthcare/waiting-time-for-orthopaedic-surgeries-increases-at-aiims-delhi/articleshow/116335019.cms?from=mdr
2 https://timesofindia.indiatimes.com/city/delhi/aiims-mri-scan-waitlist-reaches-three-years-for-most-patients/articleshow/115461193.cms

3 https://pmc.ncbi.nlm.nih.gov/articles/PMC8189845/#:~:text=India%20has%20the%20highest%20incidence,Tuberculosis%3B%202020%20%5B1%5D.

4 https://journals.lww.com/ijmr/fulltext/2024/02000/evaluation_of_prescriptions_from_tertiary_care.3.aspx

5 Apex Laboratories vs Deputy Commissioner of Income Tax SLP (Civil) NO. 23207 OF 2019

6 https://main.sci.gov.in/supremecourt/2019/33259/33259_2019_2_1501_33618_Judgement_22-Feb-2022.pdf

7 https://timesofindia.indiatimes.com/business/india-business/multivitamin-tops-drug-sales-for-1st-time-in-oct/articleshow/79768560.cms

8 https://pharmaceuticals.gov.in/sites/default/files/UCMPMD_0.pdf

9 https://pharma-dept.gov.in/sites/default/files/Apex%20Committee%20Order%20dated%2023.12.2024.pdf

10 https://www.ncbi.nlm.nih.gov/pmc/articles/PMC3657891/

11 https://www.thelancet.com/journals/lansea/article/PIIS2772-3682(22)00030-0/fulltext

12 https://ncdc.mohfw.gov.in/wp-content/uploads/2024/03/FinalNACNETReport.pdf

13 https://www.healthdata.org/sites/default/files/files/Projects/GRAM/India_0.pdf

14 https://gh.bmj.com/content/9/2/e015212

10 Medicine Beyond Borders

1 https://www.researchgate.net/publication/341600281_FACTORS_INFLUENCING_THE_METEORIC_RISE_OF_THE_INDIAN_MEDICAL_TOURISM_SECTOR_AND_ITS_IMPACT_ON_THE_ECONOMY

2 https://ijme.in/articles/medical-tourism-in-india-winners-and-losers/?galley=html

3 https://www.tbsnews.net/bangladesh/health/bmdc-bans-practice-2-indian-doctors-353605 https://www.tbsnews.net/bangladesh/health/bmdc-bans-practice-2-indian-doctors-353605?amp

4 https://www.notto.mohfw.gov.in/WriteReadData/Portal/News/867_1_2013_to_2023_updated_on_28th_July_2024__1_.pdf

5 https://www.telegraph.co.uk/global-health/science-and-disease/kidney-organ-trafficking-scandal-private-healthcare-india-myanmar/

6 https://www.ndtv.com/delhi-news/kidney-racket-busted-in-delhis-apollo-hospital-5-persons-arrested-1415359

7 https://indianexpress.com/article/express-exclusive/from-dhaka-to-delhi-how-kidney-racket-grew-on-fake-family-trees-fudged-papers-and-a-ghost-lab-9618885/
8 https://indianexpress.com/article/cities/delhi/7-held-in-kidney-transplant-racket-two-bangladeshi-nationals-stayed-in-hotel-behind-hospital-never-doubted-them-say-staff-9443515/
9 https://www.livemint.com/industry/foreign-embassies-urged-to-allot-private-hospitals-to-patients-directly-11706550400247.html
10
11 https://www.ndtv.com/andhra-pradesh-news/andhra-pradesh-auto-driver-clicks-facebook-ad-promising-rs-30-lakh-for-kidney-then-this-happens-6066875
12 https://www.facebook.com/share/p/18XVquzAaM/?mibextid=wwXIfr
13 https://timesofindia.indiatimes.com/india/health-camps-a-tool-for-private-hospitals-to-hike-occupancy/articleshow/115875971.cms
14 https://theprint.in/india/manipur-bjp-mla-attacked-by-mob-critical-in-delhi-hospital-family-claims-no-one-from-party-has-visited/1562211/
15 https://www.hindustantimes.com/mumbai-news/maharashtra-plans-law-to-ban-kickbacks-to-doctors-for-referring-patients/story-huDcy5lTqjdAxC23mFT7xN.html
16 https://blogs.bmj.com/bmj/2017/07/07/we-need-to-end-cut-practice-in-indian-healthcare/

11 The Cutting Edge

1 https://medicine.yale.edu/news/yale-medicine-magazine/article/medical-devices-and-technology-across-the-years/
2 https://gh.bmj.com/content/5/2/e002026
3 https://phfi.org/wp-content/uploads/2023/03/2023-Equitable-Access-to-Medical-Devices.pdf
4 https://www.livemint.com/companies/news/inside-the-chaos-at-pristyn-care-11693337299658.html
5 https://wbconsumers.gov.in/writereaddata/ACT%20&%20RULES/Relevant%20Act%20&%20Rules/Code%20of%20Medical%20Ethics%20Regulations.pdf
6 https://x.com/Teamtwts2/status/1808383986152231094
7 https://journals.sagepub.com/doi/full/10.1177/0272989X14556130
8 https://www.hindustantimes.com/trending/health-science-illiterate-samantha-ruth-prabhu-slammed-by-liver-doc-for-hydrogen-peroxide-nebulisation-post-101720093872072.html

9 https://www.fredhutch.org/en/news/center-news/2014/05/the-angelina-jolie-effect--one-year-later.html
10 https://www.sciencedirect.com/science/article/pii/S1098360021047481
11 https://www.nature.com/articles/s41598-021-82654-x
12 https://timesofindia.indiatimes.com/city/kolkata/bengal-woman-does-an-angelina-jolie-gets-preventive-breast-cancer-op/articleshow/79068726.cms
13 https://timesofindia.indiatimes.com/city/mumbai/ex-teacher-with-family-history-of-cancer-chooses-double-mastectomy/articleshow/47043720.cms
14 https://www.researchgate.net/publication/260130053_Angelina's_choice_private_decision_public_impact
15 https://economictimes.indiatimes.com/magazines/panache/navjot-singh-sidhu-shares-diet-and-treatment-that-helped-his-wife-beat-cancer-neem-leaves-turmeric/articleshow/115571366.cms?from=mdr
16 https://www.indiatoday.in/india/story/navjot-sidhu-wife-cancer-strict-diet-tata-memorial-oncologists-2638861-2024-11-23
17 https://diabetesjournals.org/care/article/47/Supplement_1/S231/153941/12-Retinopathy-Neuropathy-and-Foot-Care-Standards
18 https://www.cancer.gov/about-cancer/diagnosis-staging/ct-scans-fact-sheet#is-the-radiation-from-ct-harmful
19 https://www-pub.iaea.org/MTCD/Publications/PDF/Pub1532_web.pdf

12 Acing the Playbook

1 https://www.niti.gov.in/catastrophic-health-spending-and-impoverishment-households-while-seeking-hospital-treatment
2 https://nhrc.nic.in/sites/default/files/charter_patient_rights_by_NHRC_2019.pdf
3 https://x.com/mishichoudhary/status/1864963581416005980
4 https://cms.nic.in/ncdrcusersWeb/GetJudgement.do?method=GetJudgement&caseidin=0%2F0%2FRP%2F2448%2F2013&dtofhearing=2014-07-22
5 https://www.business-standard.com/article/current-affairs/patients-cannot-be-forced-to-buy-medicines-from-hospital-attached-shops-122121200427_1.html

Postscript

1 https://ibef.org/industry/healthcare-india#:~:text=Market%20Size,pharmaceuticals%20sector%20stood%20at%20Rs

Index

About the Author

Abantika Ghosh is a journalist and public policy professional who has covered the health sector for two decades, working closely with government and private stakeholders as well as public health experts. She has reported from remote parts of India for *The Times of India*, *The Indian Express*, *ThePrint* and *The Statesman*.

Her first book, *Billions Under Lockdown: The Inside Story of India's Fight Against COVID-19*, was longlisted for the Tata Literary Festival First Book Award as well as for the AutHer Award for Best Debut Author. Abantika lives in New Delhi with her three dogs.